WARD'S DAILY ALMANAC PRESENTS

THE BOOK OF MARCH

Compiled by W.B. Ward

Edited by Leslie M. Boling

ISBN 978-1453746455 EAN 1453746455

For Jim and April.

Table of Contents

FORWARD

Contrary to what one may believe from reading this book (or any one of the twelve books in its series), I have not always had a love for history. In fact, if any of my history teachers knew that I had taken on this project, they would be stunned into permanent insanity! As my son has reminded me on more than one occasion, there was so little history to study when I was a student that I had no excuse whatsoever!

It wasn't until I became a broadcaster that I first began to be intrigued by the paths that many had taken through time. At first, I became somewhat of a trivia buff. At the time it was considered quite appropriate for disc jockeys to come up with entertaining trivia questions in order to give away various trinkets to adoring listeners. One station where I had worked (KAKC; Tulsa, OK) had a morning man ("Morning Mouth McCarthy") who had a daily presentation of "Little-Less-Known-and-Little-Less-Cared-For-Facts." This was the genesis of my curiosity.

Of course this led to the eventual purchase of the popular game "Trivial Pursuit." It was through this game where I really began learning about history and its importance to everyday life.

Although the game certainly had its share of errors (as in the case of many historical collections), it still fed my curiosity and developed a philosophy of learning that I wished I had possessed while I was still in school.

Among my lessons, I learned that history truly is a living thing. It began the second I was born and will continue long after I've gone. History is simply a collection of footprints left by countless individuals as they walked over the sands of life's many beaches. Some footprints are larger than others and some are much clearer; but all footprints move in the same direction: from start to finish.

Some footprints have been declared more important than others, but that's where I tend to take issue with many educators. Yes, I see the importance of events like the signing of the Declaration of Independence, the attack on Pearl Harbor, and Columbus' famous trips. However, what I believe are important are the more mundane events of time; the invention of the beer pump handle, the first soda jerk, the day color television first became available, and so forth. The events covered in textbooks are truly important, but it is the trivial that truly make us who we have become and colors our world.

My sources of information are as varied as the facts themselves. Some of the events I found in newspapers, some in book and some in documentaries and on rare occasions, I was actually around to see the incident take place first-hand. Of course, the Internet has always provided an ample amount of information and I have verified every tidbit of information as much as humanly possible. That being said, I feel the need to make one thing abundantly clear: this body of work should only be treated as light reading. I offer it for entertainment purposes (i.e., "water cooler chat") only. Occasional, hopefully rare, errors may be present.

It is my sincerest wish that people who stumble across this book will place it in a well-known spot in their bookcase and refer to it often. It is interesting to see what happened on our various red-letter days, and to see who shares the same birthdays. Sometimes it is not enough to know the how and why, but it is occasionally important to also know the when.

This is but one of my footprints.

W.B. Ward

ABOUT THE AUTHOR

Having worked as a mentalist, W. B. Ward discovered that his effects were often based on tricks used by con men to bilk honest people from their hard-earned money. Using his craft as a springboard, he began researching various schemes to defraud unwitting victims, and he has compiled his findings into a book called Brother Can You Spare a Dime? And Other Popular Cons. In it, he reveals a myriad of

W.B. Ward

swindles, along with suggested defenses against each con. (Sadly, however, this book is currently out of print.)

Born in 1958, W. B. Ward has worked in various fields of the entertainment industry including: music, radio, television, theatre, concerts, carnivals, professional wrestling, and others.

In radio he has worked in stations coast to coast including (but not limited to): 97.5 KMOD; 101.5 the Beat; 92.1 KISS FM; KOOL 106.1; KAKC AM 1300; AM 1430 the Buzz; KMUS; KRLQ; KBIX; KGNX-TV; KRRG-FM; KRKC-FM; KNIC; and KVOO. His television credits include KGNS-TV; KOKI Fox 23; KLDO-TV; KOTV; KTUL; KJRH; ABC's *That's Incredible*; Westwood One's *PM Magazine*; and he was invited to perform on NBC's *Phenomenon*. W. B. Ward currently writes and produces a daily 2-minute feature, *Wards Daily Almanac*, which airs on stations around the country.

Playing over 30 instruments, he is also an accomplished musician. His love of performing, combined with his love for music, encouraged him into the studio where he has recorded (and is currently recording) a number of CDs.

If you would like to book W. B. Ward as a motivational speaker at your next event, meeting, or convention, send us an email to check for availability. Email all enquiries to: info@wbward.com.

For more information on W. B. Ward's books, CDs, radio programs, or personal appearances, please visit his website at: www.wbward.com.

March: The Beginning

Happy New Year! This isn't exactly the type of greeting one would expect to hear for the third month of the year, but at one time it would have been considered to have been an appropriate greeting.

Ancient Romans considered spring to be the first season of the year as this was when all things began anew. Under that old Roman calendar the month of March was the first month of spring and hence the first month of the year. It wasn't until the reign of King Numa Pompilius in 713 BC (or under the *Decemvirs*[1] about 450 BC, depending on which Roman writer one believes) when January was chosen as the first month relegating March to the third position in the year.

The name of the month also came from the Romans who declared this month in honor of Mars, the Roman god of war (second in importance to their god Jupiter, the king of the gods). It was during this month in which they held the first of two annual festivals for their god of combat (the other being in October), which also served as the springboard for their military campaigns, and it was from this Roman deity which inspired the name *Martius* which later evolved to the more familiar *March*.

Even though under King Pompilius March took third place in the year, many countries continued using March 1st as the beginning of the

---

[1] A Latin term meaning "Ten Men" which indicated a commission within the Roman Republic.

numbered year until the adaptation of the Gregorian calendar in 1752. Still to this day there are many societies and countries that celebrate the beginning of the New Year in March.

People born March 1st through the 20th are born under the astrological sign Pisces, and from the 21st Aries becomes the ruling symbol. Depending on the astrologist, people born in March are said to be natural teachers and make great philosophers. Not surprisingly, people like Alexander Graham Bell, Antonio Vivaldi, Albert Einstein and Johann Sebastian Bach all claim birthdays in March.

The birthstones for March are the aquamarine and bloodstone; both of which mean courage. The birth flower for the month is the Daffodil.

MARCH 1ST

BIRTHDAYS FOR MARCH 1ST

1810 Frédéric Chopin; composer

1904 Glenn Miller; bandleader

1910 David Niven; Academy Award-winning actor

1914 Ralph Waldo Ellison; author

1922 William Gaines; publisher

1924 Deke Slayton; astronaut

1926 Robert Clary; actor

1926 Pete Rozelle; American commissioner of the NFL

1927 Harry Belafonte; singer

1935 Robert Conrad; actor

1944 Roger Daltrey; singer

1944 John J. Breaux; U.S. Senator

1945 Dirk Benedict; actor

1947 Alan Thicke; actor

1954 Catherine Bach; actress

1954 Ron Howard; actor, director

1956 Timothy Daly; actor

1963 Ron Francis; hockey

1970 Yolanda Griffith; basketball

1973 Chris Webber; basketball

1974 Mark-Paul Gosselaar; actor

EVENTS FOR MARCH 1st

1493 - Martin Pinzon, commander of the Pinta, arrived at Bayona, Spain where Europe got its first news of the new world.

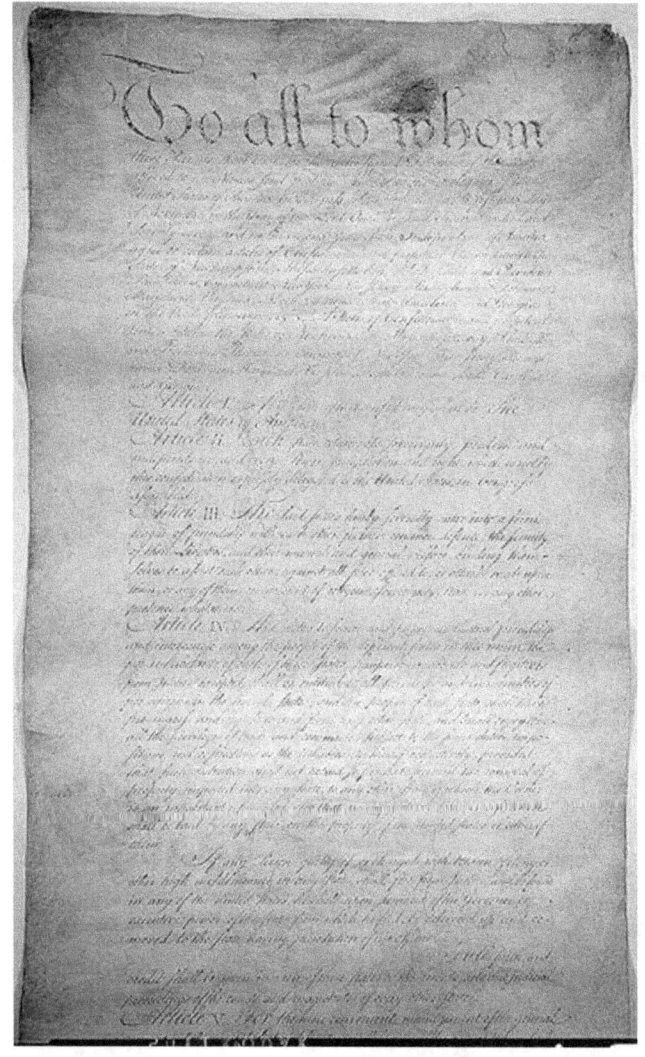

The first of 5 pages of the Articles of Confederation. Public domain.

1565 - The city of Rio de Janeiro proper was founded by the Portuguese.

1781 – The Articles of Confederation were formally ratified.

1790 - The first Census Act was passed during the second session of the first Congress and was signed by President George Washington.

1803 - Ohio was admitted as the 17th state.

1811 - Egypt's ruler Mohammed Ali (not to be confused with the boxer) massacred the leaders of the Mameluke dynasty.

1815 - Napoleon landed in France after returning from the island of Elba.

1836 – A convention of delegates from 57 Texas communities convened in Washington-on-the-Brazos, Texas, to deliberate independence from Mexico.

1845 – President John Tyler signed a bill authorizing the United States to annex the Republic of Texas.

1867 – Nebraska became the 37th U.S. state; Lancaster, Nebraska was renamed Lincoln and became the state capital.

1872 – Yellowstone National Park was established as the world's first national park.

The geyser known as "Old Faithful" erupts roughly every 91 minutes in Yellowstone National Park. Public domain.

1873 - E. Remington and Sons of Ilion, New York, began manufacturing the first practical typewriter.

1890 - *Literary Digest* was published for the first time.

1896 - Italian Forces were defeated by the Ethiopians at the Battle of Adowa, dealing a blow to Italian hopes of building an empire in Africa.

1910 – In terms of lives lost, the worst avalanche to date in United States history buried a Great Northern Railway train in northeastern King County, Washington and claimed 96 lives.

1912 - Captain Albert Berry, of the Jefferson Barracks in St. Louis, Missouri, executed the first parachute jump from a moving airplane.

1917 – The U.S. government releases the unencrypted text of the *Zimmermann Telegram* to the public. The message was a proposal from Germany to Mexico to make war against the United States.

The actual unencrypted *Zimmerman Telegram*. Public domain.

1919 - The Samil Independence Movement began in Korea, demonstrating against Japanese rule. It was also known as the March First Movement and lasted a year.

1928 - Paul Whiteman and his orchestra recorded "Ol' Man River" for Victor Records.

1932 - Charles Lindbergh Jr., the 20-month old son of aviation hero Charles Lindbergh, was kidnapped from the family's new mansion in Hopewell, New Jersey.

1936 – Hoover Dam (which was occasionally known as "Boulder Dam") was declared to be complete and was officially handed over to the United States Government.

Hoover Dam. Photo by Ansel Adams, provided by the Archival Research Catalog of the National Archives and Records Administration. Public domain.

1936 – A worker's strike occurred aboard the S.S. *California*, which led to the demise of the International Seamen's Union and the creation of the National Maritime Union.

1941 - FM Radio began in the United States with the first broadcast from W47MV (now known as WSM-FM).

1941 - Bulgaria joined the Axis Powers and allowed German forces to enter the country.

1949 – "The Brown Bomber," Joe Louis, announced he was retiring from boxing.

1949 - *Ripley's Believe it or Not* made its premiere on live television with Robert Ripley as host. Mr. Ripley made it through the first thirteen episodes before he died from a heart attack. Believe it, or not.

1950 - In Britain, Dr. Klaus Fuchs was convicted for giving British and American atomic secrets to the Soviet government.

1950 - Chiang Kai-shek resumed the presidency of the Nationalist Chinese government.

1953 – Joseph Stalin suffered a stroke and collapsed. He died four days later.

1954 - The United States announced it had conducted a hydrogen bomb test on

the Bikini Atoll in the Pacific Ocean. The device they used was called "The Castle Bravo," a 15-megaton hydrogen bomb. The resulting explosion is said to have left the worst radioactive contamination ever caused by the United States.

The mushroom cloud produced by the "Castle Bravo" detonation on the Bikini Atoll. Public domain.

1954 – The 83rd Congress was in session in Washington D.C. and was in the process of debating an immigration bill. Dissatisfied with the progress, four Puerto Rican nationalists unfurled a Puerto Rican flag from a nearby balcony and began shooting at the lawmakers. Although the hall was crowded with 240 Representatives, only five were shot and no one was killed.

1959 - Archbishop Makarios returned to Cyprus from a one-year exile.

1961 - The Peace Corps was created by an executive order from President Kennedy.

1962 – American Airlines Flight 1 crashed on take off in New York. All passengers and crew, 87 total, died on impact. One missing bolt from the jet's rudder assembly is what many think was the cause of the accident.

1966 - The Soviet spacecraft Venera III landed on Venus and became the first spacecraft to land on the surface of another planet.

1966 – The Ba'ath Party assumed power in Syria.

1968 - Country music stars, Johnny Cash and June Carter, got married. They had met some thirteen years earlier, and Johnny had proposed several times but was turned down on each occasion. His perseverance finally paid off.

1969 - Mickey Mantle announced he was retiring from baseball.

1969 – During a concert in Miami, Jim Morrison, lead singer for The Doors, was said to have "exposed himself" while in performance. Although witnesses later recanted their claims, the rock group was banned from performing at many venues.

1971 – A group called the Weathermen, an American radical left organization, took credit for a bomb that had been detonated in a men's room in the United States Capitol. In a written note, they said the bombing was in protest of the US invasion of Laos. No one was injured in the blast.

The Watergate Complex as it seen from the air. Public domain.

1974 – American Grand Jury issued indictments against President Richard Nixon's top aides. Known as the "Watergate Seven," those indicted were John N. Mitchell, H. R. Haldeman, John Ehrlichman, Charles Colson, Gordon C. Strachan, Robert Mardian, and Kenneth Parkinson. The grand jury also named President Nixon an "unindicted co-conspirator."

1989 – The United States became a member of the Berne Convention for the Protection of Literary and Artistic Works.

1992 - Bosnian Muslims and Croats voted to secede from Yugoslavia.

1995 – After about a year after its founding, the popular search engine/web portal "Yahoo!" was finally incorporated.

1999 - The Ottawa Treaty went into effect. It was a United Nations Treaty banning land mines, earlier signed by more than 130 nations.

2000 – The Constitution of Finland was rewritten.

2000 – Hans Blix assumed the position of Executive Chairman of the United Nations Monitoring, Verification and Inspection Commission (UNMOVIC).

2002 – Operation Anaconda began in eastern Afghanistan and lasted for almost three weeks.

A Chinook dropping troops during Operation Anaconda. Public domain.

2002 – The Envisat environmental satellite successfully reached an orbit 500 miles above the Earth.

2002 – The peseta was discontinued as official currency of Spain and was replaced with the euro (€).

2003 – Management of the United States Customs Service and the United States Secret Service was moved to the United States Department of Homeland Security.

2003 – The International Criminal Court held its inaugural session in The Hague.

2005 – The death penalty for juveniles was found to be unconstitutional in America.

2007 – Tornadoes swarmed across the southern United States, killing at least 20; eight of the deaths were at a high school in Enterprise, Alabama.

2007 – "Squatters" were evicted from Ungdomshuset in Copenhagen, Denmark, provoking the March 2007 Denmark Riots.

BIRTHDAYS FOR MARCH 2nd

1793 Sam Houston; President of Republic of Texas, U.S. Senator, Texas governor

1810 Pope Leo XIII (Giocchino Vincenzo Pecci); 256th pope of the Roman Catholic Church

1816 Alexander H. Bullock; 26th Governor of Massachusetts

1876 Pope Pius XII; pope of the Roman Catholic Church

1904 Dr. Seuss (Theodor Seuss Geisel); Pulitzer Prize-winning author

1909 Mel Ott; American baseball player

1917 Desi Arnaz (Desiderio Alberto Arnez y de Acha III); bandleader, singer, actor

1930 John Cullum; singer, actor

1931 Mikhail Gorbachev; President of the Soviet Union

1931 Tom Wolfe; author

1932 Chico Fernandez; baseball

1942 John Irving; author

1944 Lou Reed; singer, songwriter, guitarist

1949 Gates McFadden; American actress

1950 Karen Carpenter; drummer, Grammy Award-winning singer

1952 Laraine Newman; comedienne, actress

1953 Russell D. Feingold; U.S. Senator

1955 Jay Osmond; singer

1956 John Cowsill; singer

1956 Mark Evans; musician, bassist

1962 Jon Bon Jovi (John Francis Bongiovi); singer, musician, songwriter

1964 Mike Von Erich; American wrestler

EVENTS FOR MARCH 2nd

1776 - In advance of the Continental Army's occupation of Dorchester Heights, Massachusetts, General George Washington ordered American artillery forces to begin bombarding Boston from their positions at Lechmere Point, northwest of the city center. Ten days later the eight-year British occupation of Boston ended when British troops evacuated the city.

1791 – Semaphore, the ability to send messages by holding a pair of flags, became mechanized. A semaphore machine was developed in Paris which allowed messages to be sent over a greater distance.

1836 - Texas adopted their Declaration of Independence from Mexico.

Chappe telegraf at Louvre, Paris. Public domain.

1877 - Just two days before inauguration, the U.S. Congress declared Rutherford B. Hayes the winner of the presidential election even though Samuel J. Tilden had won the popular vote on November 7, 1876.

1882 - Roderick McLean attempted to assassinate Queen Victoria of The United Kingdom on March 2, 1882 at Windsor, with a pistol. Roderick failed.

1887 - The American Trotting Association was formed in Detroit, Michigan.

1899 – Mount Rainier National Park was established.

Mount Ranier. Creative Commons License; used by permission.

1903 - In New York City, the Martha Washington Hotel opened for business. It was the first hotel exclusively for women. As of 2003, the hotel was still standing and operating under the name "Hotel Thirty Thirty" (named for its address at 30 E. 30th).

1925 - State and federal highway officials appointed the Joint Board on Interstate Highways which designed the now familiar "shield" marker bearing the United States Highway numbers.

1933 – The film *King Kong* opened at Radio City Music Hall and the RKO Roxy; both in New York City. Each showing was preceded by a lavish stage show and tickets ranged from 35-cents to 75-cents.

1937 – The Steel Workers Organizing Committee signed a collective bargaining agreement with U.S. Steel, which led to the unionization of the United States steel industry.

1939 – Cardinal Eugenio Pacelli was elected Pope and assumed the name Pius XII.

1940 - The first, televised, intercollegiate track meet was broadcast to viewers in New York City, courtesy of W2XBS (today that station is known as WNBC).

1944 – *The Academy Awards'* presentation moved from a banquet hall to Grauman's Chinese Theatre in Los Angeles, California. The move afforded the presentations to take on a more theatric appearance rather than being held in banquet halls. The award for Best Picture went to *Casa Blanca*.

Grauman's Chinese Theatre. Photo provided by the United States Library of Congress's Prints and Photographs division. Public domain.

1944 - A train stopped in a tunnel near Salerno, Italy, and more than 500 people on board suffocated and died. The details were sketchy, but some have suggested the overloaded train stopped inside the tunnel to avoid skidding on the rain-soaked tracks that were on a steep upgrade outside the tunnel. The train was burning low-grade coal substitutes that emitted an odorless and colorless carbon monoxide. Suffocation of everyone on board barely took 30 minutes.

1946 - Ho Chi Minh was elected president of North Vietnam.

1949 - Capt. James Gallagher completed the first non-stop round the world flight. He completed the 23,452-mile flight in 94 hours 1 minute.

1949 - The first automatic streetlight system, in which the streetlights turned themselves on at dark, was installed in New Milford, Connecticut.

1956 - Morocco's independence was recognized by France.

1958 - Dr. Vivian Fuchs completed the first crossing of Antarctica by land.

1962 – Wilt Chamberlain set the single-game scoring record in the National Basketball Association by scoring 100 points. Chamberlain led Philadelphia to defeat New York 169-147.

1964 - Shooting began on The Beatles' first feature film *A Hard Day's Night*. One scene in the movie featured the Beatles in concert in front of an audience filled with extras. Among those in attendance was a then 13-year old future recording artist Phil Collins.

1965 – The US and South Vietnamese Air Force began "Operation Rolling Thunder," a sustained bombing campaign against North Vietnam.

1966 - The Ford Motor Company celebrated the production of its one-millionth Mustang, a white convertible.

1969 – The first of two prototype *Concordes* made its maiden flight from Toulouse. *Concorde* 001 made its first test flight piloted by Andre Turcat.

The *Concorde* **216. Public domain.**

1972 - The United States spacecraft Pioneer 10 was launched; it passed close by Jupiter and Neptune before leaving the solar system.

1974 - Stevie Wonder was awarded five Grammy Awards for his album, *Innervisions* and his songs, "You Are the Sunshine of My Life" and "Superstition".

1974 - Postage stamps for first-class mail jumped from 8 to 10 cents.

1978 – Czech Vladimír Remek became the first non-Russian or non-American to go into space, when he was launched aboard Soyuz 28.

1978 – Two men stole the corpse of the revered film

Charlie Chaplin circa 1910. Public domain.

actor Sir Charles Chaplin from a cemetery in the Swiss village of Corsier-sur-Vevey, located in the hills above Lake Geneva, near Lausanne, Switzerland. Two auto mechanics were eventually arrested for the crime after they led police to a shallow grave where they had buried the actor's corpse. Chaplin had been dead since 1977.

1986 - Queen Elizabeth signed the Australia Act, formally severing the last constitutional ties between Britain and Australia.

1987 - Two sets of quintuplets were born, one set to Rosalind Helms in Peoria, Illinois, and another set to Robin Jenkins of Las Vegas, Nevada.

1990 - In South Africa, Nelson Mandela was elected deputy president of the African National Congress.

1995 - Seven-time Italian Prime Minister Giulio Andreotti was ordered to stand trial on charges of having been a member of the Mafia.

1996 - Paul Keating's Labor Party suffered a defeat in Australian elections, ending 13 years of rule.

1998 – Data sent from the Galileo spacecraft indicated that Jupiter's moon Europa has a liquid ocean under a thick crust of ice.

1999 - Dusty Springfield, singer of 1960's pop songs ("Wishin' and Hopin'," "The Look of Love") and the signature bluesy classic, "Son of a Preacher Man," lost her battle to breast

Galileo being prepped before initial launch. Public domain.

cancer.

2003 – The first International Symposium on Taiwan Sign Language Linguistics was held at Chung Cheng University.

2004 – Voters in the U.S. state of Georgia voted on a referendum concerning its Confederacy-derived flag. The official state flag of the Peach State currently contains no visual reference to the Confederacy.

2004 – Al Qaeda carried out the Ashoura Massacre in Iraq, killing 170 and wounding over 500.

2008 – Riots in Yerevan, Armenia concerning the Armenian presidential election of 2008, came to a fatal end, with police forces clashing with civilians in their peaceful protest, resulting in eight deaths.

MARCH 3ʳᵈ

BIRTHDAYS FOR MARCH 3ʳᵈ

1831 George Pullman; inventor, industrialist

1847 Alexander Graham Bell; teacher of the deaf, inventor

1911 Jean Harlow; actress

1920 James Doohan; actor

1921 Diana Barrymore; actress

1923 Doc Watson; American musician

1947 Jennifer Warnes; American singer and songwriter

1950 Tim Kazurinsky; actor, comedian, writer

1952 Randy Gradishar; football

1958 Mianda Richardson; actress

1962 Herschel Walker; football

1962 Jackie Joyner-Kersee; Olympic gold medalist

1966 Tone-Loc; rap singer

1974 David Faustino; actor

1982 Jessica Biel; actress

EVENTS FOR MARCH 3ʳᵈ

1585 – The Olympic Theatre, designed by Andrea Palladio, was inaugurated in Vicenza with a production of Sophocles' *Oedipus the King*.

Ward's Daily Almanac; The Book of March page 29

Oil painting depicting the Battle of Nassau. Public domain.

1776 – The first amphibious landing of the Continental Navy and the Continental Marines (forerunners of the United States Navy and the United States Marine Corps) kicked-off the Battle of Nassau.

1845 - Florida was admitted as the 27th state.

1845 - Congress reined in President John Tyler's zealous use of the presidential veto, overriding it with the necessary two-thirds vote. This marked Congress' first use of the Constitutional provision allowing Congressional veto overrides and represented Congress' parting gift to Tyler as he left office.

1849 – The U.S. Congress passed the "Gold Coinage Act" which allowed the minting of gold coins.

1873 - Congress enacted the so-called Comstock Law, making it illegal to send any "obscene, lewd, or lascivious" book through the mail.

1875 – Indoor ice hockey makes its public debut in Montreal, Quebec with the inaugural indoor hockey game being played in the Victoria Skating Rink. Up until then, hockey was played as an outdoor sport with no set dimensions for the ice and no rules regarding the number of players. This first indoor game was played with 9 players on each side.

1887 – Anne Sullivan Macy began teaching six-year-old Helen Keller, who lost her sight and hearing after a severe illness at the age of 19 months.

1875 - The first performance of French composer George Bizet's opera *Carmen* took place at the Opera Comique, Paris.

1878 - The peace treaty at San Stefano was signed, ending the Russo-Turkish War and gaining independence for Serbia.

Anne Sullivan Macy circa 1887. Public domain.

1879 – The United States Geological Survey, an organization to study the landscape of the United States, its natural resources, and the natural hazards that threaten it, was created.

1879 – Belva Ann Bennett Lockwood became the first woman lawyer to be admitted to appear before the Supreme Court of the United States.

Photo of Belva Ann Bennett Lockwood taken by Matthew Brady. Public domain.

1885 – The American Telephone & Telegraph Company was incorporated in New York.

1886 - The Treaty of Bucharest was signed, bringing peace between Bulgaria and Serbia.

1913 - Marchers in a parade held by the National American Woman Suffrage Association in Washington D.C. were attacked. When Genevieve Stone, wife of Congressman William J. Stone (MO), asked a policeman for protection, he reportedly answered, "If my wife were you, I'd break her head."

1915 – National Advisory Committee for Aeronautics (NACA), the predecessor of NASA, was founded.

The first cover of *Time Magazine*. Public domain

1915 - A few weeks after its West Coast premiere in Los Angeles, a 40-piece orchestra accompanied D.W. Griffith's controversial Civil War epic, *The Birth of a Nation,* in New York City.

1923 – The first issue of *Time Magazine* was published. The cover displayed the Speaker of the United States House of Representatives, Joseph Gurney Cannon.

1931 - Cab Calloway and his

orchestra recorded "Minnie the Moocher" for the first time.

1931 – "The Star-Spangled Banner," written by Francis Scott Key, became the official national anthem of the United States.

1939 - A new craze swept college campuses and it all began at Harvard University. Accepting a dare, a freshman named Lothrop Withington, Junior tilted back his head and swallowed a live goldfish. And so the stupidity began.

1943 - In World War II, 178 people were killed in an accident at an air raid shelter in London's Bethnal Green. The incident occurred when the crowd inside the shelter suddenly lunged forward in response to an air raid. Within seconds a crowd of 300 people were crushed against each other in a small stairwell and a total of 172 people died.

1951 - Don Herbert, as "Mr. Wizard," began performing experiments on the NBC series of the same name which ran for 14 continuous years.

1959 – As a result of a "name-the-park" contest, the San Francisco Giants baseball team's new home was officially named Candlestick Park.

The original configuration of Candlestick Park in a photo from about 1960. Public domain.

1963 - A new constitution was approved in Senegal under which the president took over the powers of the prime minister.

1969 - The three-man Apollo 9 spacecraft, used to test the lunar module, was launched from Cape Kennedy.

1974 - A DC-10 jet crashed into a forest outside of Paris, France, killing all 346 people on board. The crash was due to a poorly latched cargo door that blew off the plane at 11,000 feet.

1977 - Singer Bing Crosby fell 20 feet into the orchestra pit at the Ambassador Auditorium in Pasadena, California, after taping a CBS television special.

1980 – After more than 25 years of service, the USS *Nautilus* was decommissioned and stricken from the Naval Vessel Register. Besides being the first to travel underneath the North Pole, the Nautilus was also the world's first nuclear powered submarine.

1985 - Cybill Shepherd and Bruce Willis starred in the premiere of ABC's comedy-adventure, *Moonlighting*.

1987 - At age 74, Danny Kaye, died in Los Angeles, California.

1991 – An amateur video captured the beating of Rodney King by Los Angeles police officers. A little more than a year later, the trial in which four LAPD officers were acquitted for the beating led to the 1992 Los Angeles riots.

1991 – United Airlines Flight 585 crashed on approach into Colorado Springs, Colorado, killing 25. Among the dead, Patricia Edison: the first female pilot to die in an accident involving a United States jet airliner.

1996 – Spain's conservative Popular Party claimed victory in general elections to end 13 years of Socialist rule under Prime Minister Felipe Gonzalez. It was this election which named Don José María Aznar as Prime Minister of Spain.

**Spanish Prime Minister José Maria Aznar.
Public domain.**

1997 – The tallest free-standing structure in the Southern Hemisphere, Sky Tower in downtown Auckland, New Zealand, opened after two-and-a-half years of construction.

2004 – Belgian brewer Interbrew and Brazilian rival AmBev agreed to merge in an $11.2 billion deal that formed InBev, the world's largest brewer to date.

2005 – James Roszko murdered four Royal Canadian Mounted Police constables during a drug bust at his property in Rochfort Bridge, Alberta, then committed suicide. It was the deadliest peace-time incident for the RCMP since 1885 and the North-West Rebellion.

2005 – Steve Fossett became the first person to fly an airplane non-stop around the world solo without refueling.

2009 – The Sri Lankan cricket team was attacked by terrorists while on their way to the Gaddafi Stadium, Lahore for a Test match against Pakistan.

2009 – The building of the Historisches Archiv der Stadt Köln (Historical Archives) in Cologne, Germany, collapsed. It was believed that construction of a nearby subway contributed to the collapse.

BIRTHDAYS FOR MARCH 4th

1678 Antonio Vivaldi; Italian composer

1876 Theodore Hardeen (Ferencz Deszo Weis); magician, brother of Harry Houdini

1880 Channing Pollock; American playwright and critic

1888 Knute Rockne; College Football Hall of Famer, coach

1895 Shemp Howard; American comedian

1913 John Garfield; actor

1934 Barbara McNair; singer, TV hostess, actress

1938 Paula Prentiss (Ragusa); actress

1942 Gloria Gaither; American gospel songwriter

1944 Bobby Womack; songwriter

1953 Emilio Estefan; percussionist

1954 Catherine O'Hara; actress

1954 Adrian Zmed; actor

1958 Patricia Heaton; actress

1961 Ray (Boom Boom) Mancini; middleweight boxer

1961 Steven Weber; actor

1966 Kevin Maurice Johnson; basketball, Mayor of Sacramento, California

1967 Evan Dando; musician

1968 Patsy Kensit; actress

1969 Chastity (Chaz) Bono; singer, daughter of Sonny & Cher

EVENTS FOR FEBRUARY 4th

**A depiction of the *Niña* (center) by Gustav Adolf Closs.
Public domain.**

1493 – Explorer Christopher Columbus arrived back in Lisbon, Portugal aboard his ship *Niña* from his voyage to what is now the Bahamas and other islands in the Caribbean.

1681 - King Charles II of England granted a royal charter, deed, and governorship of Pennsylvania to William Penn.

1789 - The 1st Congress under the Constitution met at New York, NY.

1791 - Vermont became the 14th state.

1793 - George Washington was inaugurated in Philadelphia for a second term as president of the United States.

1797 – In the first ever peaceful transfer of power between elected leaders in modern times, John Adams was sworn in as President of the United States, succeeding George Washington.

1801 - Thomas Jefferson was inaugurated as the third president of the United States.

1837 – Chicago was incorporated as a city.

1861 – First national flag of the Confederate States of America (the "Stars and Bars") was adopted.

First national flag of the Confederate States of America. Public domain.

1861 - Abraham Lincoln was inaugurated.

1865 - Abraham Lincoln was inaugurated (2nd term).

1877 - Tchaikovsky's ballet *Swan Lake* was first performed at the Bolshoi Theatre in Moscow.

1881 – Eliza Ballou Garfield became the first mother of a United States President to live in the White House when her son, James Garfield, was inaugurated.

President Garfield (second from right) and his official family portrait. His mother is presumably the 4th from the right. From the United States Library of Congress; public domain.

1902 - The American Automobile Association (AAA) was organized.

1913 - Woodrow Wilson was inaugurated as the 28th United States President.

1918 – The first case of Spanish flu occurred in the United States (first observed in Ft. Riley, KS), and was the start of a devastating worldwide pandemic.

1925 - In the first radio broadcast of a presidential inauguration, Calvin Coolidge took the oath of office in Washington DC.

1927 – With the firing of a gun as a signal, some 25,000 diggers participated in a rush to stake their claims in new diamond fields at Grasfontein, South Africa.

1930 - Emma Fahning became the first woman bowler to achieve a perfect score while competing in a game sanctioned by the Women's International Bowling Congress.

1933 – Frances Perkins became the first woman appointed as a cabinet member. She was made Secretary of Labor by President Franklin D. Roosevelt.

1933 - Franklin D. Roosevelt was sworn in as 32nd United States president and the first, and only candidate, to be elected for a third and fourth term.

1942 - In response to a request from President Franklin D. Roosevelt to provide morale and recreation services to U.S. uniformed military personnel, the United Service Organization (better known as the USO) was formed.

1943 - Actress Greer Garson's acceptance speech for the Best Actress Academy award for her role in *Mrs. Miniver* lasted 5½ minutes, an industry record. Presently, award recipients are given time limits on their acceptance speeches.

1950 - Walt Disney released Cinderella; the first full-length, animated feature film in eight years.

1952 – Nancy Davis and Ronald Reagan were married at the Little Brown Church in the San Fernando Valley in California.

Ronald and Nancy Reagan, circa 1964.
Public domain.

1954 – Peter Bent Brigham Hospital in Boston, Massachusetts, announces the first successful kidney transplant after a kidney had been successfully moved from one identical twin to another.

1957 – The S&P 500 stock market index was introduced, replacing the S&P 90.

1962 – The United States Atomic Energy Commission announced that the first atomic power plant at the McMurdo Station in Antarctica was in operation.

1964 - United Nations Security Council adopted a resolution to appoint a mediator and establish a U.N. peacekeeping force in Cyprus.

1966 - *The London Evening Standard* published an interview with the Beatles in which John Lennon made his infamous statement, "We're more popular than Jesus." Some considered this to be the semi-official end of "Beatlemania."

1970 - The French submarine Eurydice exploded and sank off the coast of Toulon in the Mediterranean. All 57 aboard died. The cause of the explosion has never been determined.

1971 - Canadian Prime Minister Pierre Trudeau quietly married Margaret Sinclair.

1974 - *People Magazine* was officially launched. The cover featured a photo of Mia Farrow.

1974 - In Britain, Prime Minister Edward Heath resigned and Labour leader Harold Wilson formed a new government.

1975 – Actor Charlie Chaplin was knighted at Buckingham Palace.

1976 – The supercomputer known as "Cray-1" was delivered to the Los Alamos National Laboratory, New Mexico.

1977 - More than 1,570 people were killed in Romania by an earthquake which registered 7.2 on the Richter scale; 35,000 families were made homeless.

1981 - At age 84, lyricist, E.Y. "Yip" Harburg died in an auto accident in Hollywood, California. Two of his biggest hits were "Over the Rainbow" and "It's Only a Paper Moon."

1985 – The Food and Drug Administration approved a blood test for AIDS, and it has been used since then for screening all blood donations in the United States.

1986 - *Today* debuted in London as England's newest, national, daily newspaper. It had staff of 550 people, as compared to the staff of 6,000 at the *London Daily Express*.

1986 - Writer and champion of women's rights, Ding Ling (a Wade-Giles romanization Ting Ling, pseudonym of Jiang Wei), died at the age of 81 in Beijing, China.

1986 – The Vega 1, a Soviet based space probe, began returning images of Comet Halley and the first images ever of its nucleus.

1990 - President Lennox Sebe was ousted in a military coup in the South African homeland of Ciskei.

1990 – Loyola Marymount University All-American basketball player Hank Gathers died on the court of a heart attack during a conference semifinal game.

1991 - The Soviet parliament ratified a six-nation treaty (the "Two Plus Four Treaty"), setting the legal seal on German unification after two years of revolutionary change in central Europe.

1991 - Crown Prince Sheikh Saad al-Abdulla al-Sabah became the first senior member of the Kuwaiti ruling family to return to the homeland liberated from Iraqi occupation.

1994 - Four Muslim fundamentalists (Salameh, Nidal Ayyad, Mahmud Abouhalima, and Ahmad Ajaj) were found guilty of bombing the landmark World Trade Center in New York.

1994 – Space shuttle *Columbia* (STS-62) launched into orbit to conduct microgravity experiments in the shuttle's opened cargo bay.

The crew of the *Columbia* (STS-62). Standing from left to right Charles D. Gemar, Marsha S. Ivins, and Pierre J. Thuot, Seated from left to right Andrew M. Allen, pilot; and John H. Casper, commander. Public domain.

1996 - A Muslim suicide bomber killed 13 people and wounded 100, including children, outside a crowded Tel Aviv shopping mall. The bomb was described as a 20-kilogram nail bomb.

1996 - Sarah Ophelia Colley Cannon, better known as "Minnie Pearl," died of complications in Nashville, Tennessee following a stroke. She was 83 years old.

1998 – The Supreme Court of the United States ruled that federal laws banning on-the-job sexual harassment also apply when both parties are the same sex.

2001 – A massive car bomb exploded in front of the BBC Television Centre in London, seriously injuring 11 people. The attack was attributed to the Real IRA.

2001 – A bridge collapsed in northern Portugal, killing at least 70 people.

2002 – Canada banned human embryo cloning but permitted government-funded scientists to use embryos left over from fertility treatment or abortions.

2002 – Seven American Special Operations Forces soldiers were killed as they attempted to infiltrate the Shahi Kot Valley on a low-flying helicopter reconnaissance mission.

2005 – The car of released Italian hostage Giuliana Sgrena (an Italian journalist who worked for the Italian communist newspaper *Il Manifesto*) was fired on by US soldiers after it ran a roadblock in Iraq, causing the death of an Italian Secret Service Agent and injuring two passengers.

2005 – Martha Stewart was released from a federal prison near Alderson, West Virginia, after serving five months for lying about her sale of ImClone stock in 2001.

2006 – Final contact attempted with Pioneer 10 by the Deep Space Network. No response was received.

2007 – Approximately 30,000 voters took advantage of electronic voting in Estonia, the world's first nationwide voting where part of the vote casting was allowed in the form of remote electronic voting via the Internet.

2009 – The International Criminal Court (ICC) issued an arrest warrant for Sudanese President Omar Hassan al-Bashir for war crimes and crimes against humanity in Darfur. Al-Bashir was the first sitting head of state to be indicted by the ICC since its establishment in 2002.

MARCH 5th

BIRTHDAYS FOR MARCH 5th

1512 Gerardus Mercator; cartographer/geographer

1927 Jack (John Joseph Edward) Cassidy; actor

1935 Paul Sand; Tony Award-winning actor

1936 Dean Stockwell; actor

1939 Samantha Eggar; actress

1946 Michael Warren; actor

1947 Eddie Hodges; singer, actor

1947 John Kitzhaber; Governor of Oregon

1948 Eddy Grant; singer, songwriter

1950 Eugene Fodor; musician, violinist

1955 Marsha Warfield; actress, comedienne

1955 Penn Jillette; magician

1958 Andy Gibb; singer

1963 Joel Osteen; pastor and best selling author

EVENTS FOR MARCH 5th

1623 - The first temperance law in the United States was enacted in what is now known as Virginia.

1750 - The first known Shakespearean play presented in America was performed at the Nassau Street Theatre in New York City. The play presented was *King Richard III.*

1770 – The "Boston massacre" occurred when five people were killed after British troops opened fire on a crowd.

1836 - Samuel Colt made the first pistol, a .34-caliber "Texas" model.

1868 – Pursuant to a resolution drafted by Congress almost a month earlier, a court of impeachment is organized in the United States Senate to hear charges against President Andrew Johnson.

An engraving of the Boston Massacre made by Paul Revere. Public domain.

1872 - George Westinghouse patented the air brake for trains.

1912 – Italian forces were the first to use airships for military purposes, employing them for reconnaissance behind Turkish lines.

1916 - The Spanish liner *Principe de Asturias* struck a rock off the coast of Brazil and sank in minutes, killing 445 people out of the 588 aboard.

1923 - Old-age pension laws were enacted in Montana.

1924 - Frank Caruana of Buffalo, New York, became the first bowler to roll two perfect games in a row and make 29 consecutive strikes.

1933 – During the Great Depression, President Franklin D. Roosevelt declared a "bank holiday," which closed all U.S. banks and froze all financial transactions.

1933 - The German federal election was held in the Weimar Republic. Thanks to the success of the Nazi Party and its allies in the poll, its leader and Chancellor of Germany, Adolf Hitler, was able to pass the "Enabling Act," which effectively gave him the power of a dictator.

1936 – The *Spitfire* fighter plane went on show for the first time in Southampton, England.

A *Spitfire Mk IX* flown by the late Ray Hanna at Flying Legends 2005. Photo by Bryan Fury. Creative Commons License; used by permission.

1945 - In World War II an advance force of the United States 1st Army entered Cologne.

1945 - German boys as young as 16-years old were required to enroll in the regular armed forces.

1946 - Winston Churchill delivered his famous "Iron Curtain Speech" at Westminster College, Missouri.

1960 - After two years in the United States Army, Elvis Presley returned to civilian life.

1963 - The Hula-Hoop, a hip-swiveling toy that became a huge fad across America when it was first marketed by Wham-O in 1958, was patented by the company's co-founder, Arthur "Spud" Melin.

1963 - Patsy Cline, Cowboy Copas, and Hawkshaw Hawkins were killed in a single-engine plane crash near Camden, Tennessee.

1966 - Staff Sergeant Barry Sadler hit the #1 position on the music charts with "The Ballad Of The Green Berets."

1969 - The rock magazine, *Creem* was published for the first time.

1975 – The first meeting of the Homebrew Computer Club was held in Gordon French's garage in Menlo Park, San Mateo County, California. Several high-profile

A newsletter dated Sept,'76 for the Homebrew Computer Club. Public domain.

computer programmers sprang from this small hobbyist organization including the founders of Apple Computers.

1977 - The *Dial-a-President Radio Program*, featuring President Jimmy Carter and CBS news anchorman Walter Cronkite, aired for the first and only time.

1978 – The Landsat 3 satellite was launched from Vandenberg Air Force Base in California.

1979 – America's Voyager 1 spacecraft made its closest approach to Jupiter at an altitude of about 172,000 miles.

1982 - Comedian John Belushi died of a drug overdose.

1983 - The Australian Labor Party, headed by Robert Hawke, was swept into power, beating the Liberals of Malcolm Fraser.

1989 - Time Inc. and Warner Communications Inc. announced that they would merge into a world-leading media and entertainment giant.

1994 - White House lawyer Bernard Nussbaum resigned, becoming the first casualty of the Whitewater affair that had plagued the Clinton administration.

1996 - Former Bangladesh President Khondaker Mostaq Ahmad died at age 77.

2001 – In Mecca, 35 Muslim pilgrims were crushed to death during the annual Hajj pilgrimage.

2003 – In Haifa, 17 Israeli civilians were killed by a Hamas suicide bomb in the Haifa Bus 37 Massacre.

MARCH 6th

BIRTHDAYS FOR MARCH 6th

1475 Michelangelo (de Lodovico Buonarroti Simoni); artist

1619 Cyrano De Bergerac; French soldier, author

1806 Elizabeth Barrett Browning (Moulton); poet

1905 Bob Wills; fiddler, composer, bandleader

1906 Lou Costello (Louis Francis Cristillo); comedian, actor

1923 Ed McMahon; radio/TV announcer, pitchman

1924 Sarah Caldwell; conductor

1926 Alan Greenspan; economist

1927 Gordon Cooper; U.S. astronaut

1927 Gabriel Garcia-Marquez; author

1936 Marion Barry; infamous re-elected mayor of Washington, D.C.

1937 Valentina Tereshkova; Russian cosmonaut

1937 Cookie Rojas; baseball

1939 Christopher Samuel "Kit" Bond; U.S. Senator

1947 Rob Reiner; Emmy Award-winning Actor

1947 Kiki Dee (Pauline Matthews); singer

1947 Dick Fosbury; Olympic Gold Medalist, National Track & Field Hall of Famer

1959 Tom Arnold; actor

1964 Skip Ewing; American country music singer and songwriter

1969 Amy Pietz; actress

1972 Shaquille Rashaun O'Neal; basketball

1976 Ken Anderson (Mr. Kennedy); American professional wrestler

EVENTS FOR MARCH 6th

1808 - Harvard University founded the "Pierian Society," the oldest college musical club. Although somewhat debatable, some look at this as being the first college formed orchestra.

1820 – "The Missouri Compromise" was signed into law by President James Monroe. The compromise allowed Missouri to enter the Union as a slave state, but left the rest of the northern part of the Louisiana Purchase territory slavery-free.

1834 – The city of Toronto was incorporated with William Lyon Mackenzie as its first mayor.

1836 - The siege of the Alamo ended when Mexican troops under Santa Anna captured the mission fort garrisoned by Davey Crockett and 187 Texans.

1840 – Baltimore College of Dental Surgery Opened, the first Dental College in the world.

1869 – Dmitri Mendeleev presented the first periodic table of elements to the Russian Chemical Society.

1886 - *The Nightingale*, the first magazine published for nurses debuted in New York City.

1896 - Charles B. King tested his automobile on the streets of Detroit, Michigan, becoming the first man to drive a car in the Motor City. Being a thoughtful citizen, Mr. King scheduled his test after 11pm so as to not frighten horses or other citizens.

1899 – Bayer registered "aspirin" as a trademark.

1930 - Davidson's Market and Bakery in Springfield, MA became the first store to sell frozen meals. This forerunner version of the "TV-Dinner" was pre-packaged frozen foods manufactured by Clarence Birdseye.

1945 - Tanks and infantry of the United States First Army drove into Cologne, Germany.

1947 – At Newport News, Virginia, the ship USS *Newport News* was launched and was the first air-conditioned naval ship.

The USS *Newport News* at sea. Public domain.

1951 - The trial of Ethel and Julius Rosenberg began in New York Southern District federal court. Judge Irving R. Kaufman presided over the espionage prosecution of the couple accused of selling nuclear secrets to the Russians (treason could not be charged because the United States was not at war with the Soviet Union). The trial lasted nearly a month, finally ending on April 4th with convictions for all the defendants. The Rosenbergs were sentenced to death row on April 6th.

1953 - Georgy Malenkov succeeded Stalin as premier and first secretary of the Soviet Communist Party.

1957 - Ghana became an independent country within the Commonwealth.

1964 – Nation of Islam's Elijah Muhammad officially gave boxing champion Cassius Clay the name Muhammad Ali.

1967 - Svetlana Alliluyeva, Stalin's daughter, requested asylum at the United States embassy in New Delhi.

This is the very camera used by Abraham Zapruder to film the assassination of President Kennedy. (Please note the FBI identification sticker.) Photo courtesy of the U.S. National Archives.

1975 – For the first time, ever, the Zapruder film of the assassination of John F. Kennedy was shown in motion to a national TV audience by Robert J. Groden and Dick Gregory. The showing was on an ABC program hosted by Geraldo Rivera called Goodnight America.

1981 - Walter Cronkite said "And that's the way it is" for the last time, as he closed the *CBS Evening News with Walter Cronkite*. This broadcast ended a 19-year run for the award-winning journalist.

1983 - The United States Football League started its first season of professional football competition. The league would barely last five years.

1983 - Chancellor Helmut Kohl and his Christian Democrats were returned to power in Germany.

1987 - A Townsend Thoreson ferry, the MS *Herald of Free Enterprise*, capsized on its way out of Zeebrugge harbor in Belgium; 193 people drowned.

The MS Herald of Free Enterprise shown here in Dover's Eastern Docks, circa 1984. Public domain.

1987 - The comedy/drama *Lethal Weapon* opened in United States theaters.

1988 - Three members of an Irish Republican Army unit were shot dead in a Gibraltar street by undercover SAS commandos.

1992 - The president of Azerbaijan, Ayaz Mutalibov, resigned over his handling of the conflict in Nagorno-Karabakh.

1992 - A computer virus called "Michelangelo" struck thousands of personal computers around the world.

2001 - Napster, Inc., the peer-to-peer file sharing network, began complying with a Federal court order to block the transfer of copyrighted material over its web site, and this event marked the beginning of their demise. By 2002 an American bankruptcy judge ordered Napster to liquidate all of its assets according to Chapter 7 of the U.S. bankruptcy laws. The company went through a few sales until 2008 when it was purchased for $121 million by the electronics retailer Best Buy.

2006 – South Dakota Governor Mike Rounds signed legislation which banned most abortions in his state.

2007 – Former White House aide I. Lewis Libby, Jr. was found guilty on four of five counts of perjury and obstruction of justice.

MARCH 7th

BIRTHDAYS FOR MARCH 7th

1707 Stephen Hopkins; governor, signer of the Declaration of Independence

1875 Maurice Ravel; composer

1917 Lee Young; jazz musician, drummer

1923 Mahlon Clark; musician, reeds instrumentalist

1927 James Broderick; actor

1934 Willard Scott; weatherman

1938 Homero Blancas; golf

1938 Janet Guthrie; auto racer, International Women's Sports Hall of Famer

1940 Daniel J. Travanti; Emmy Award-Winning actor

1942 Tammy Faye Bakker; TV evangelist

1942 Michael Eisner; Disney executive

1945 John Heard; actor

1946 Peter Wolf (Blankfield); singer

1950 Franco Harris; Pro Football Hall of Famer

1950 Bernie MacNeil; hockey

1950 Billy Joe DuPree; football

1951 Jeff Burroughs; baseball

1952 Lynn Swann; football, TV sportscaster

1960 Ivan Lendl; tennis

1960 Joseph Carter; baseball

1962 Taylor Dayne; singer

1964 Wanda Sykes; American actress and comedienne

EVENTS FOR MARCH 7*th*

1793 – France declared war on Spain during the French Revolutionary and Napoleonic Wars.

1838 – Jenny Lind, the "Swedish Nightingale," made her debut at the Stockholm Opera.

1854 - Charles Miller received patent #10,609 for a sewing machine that stitched buttonholes.

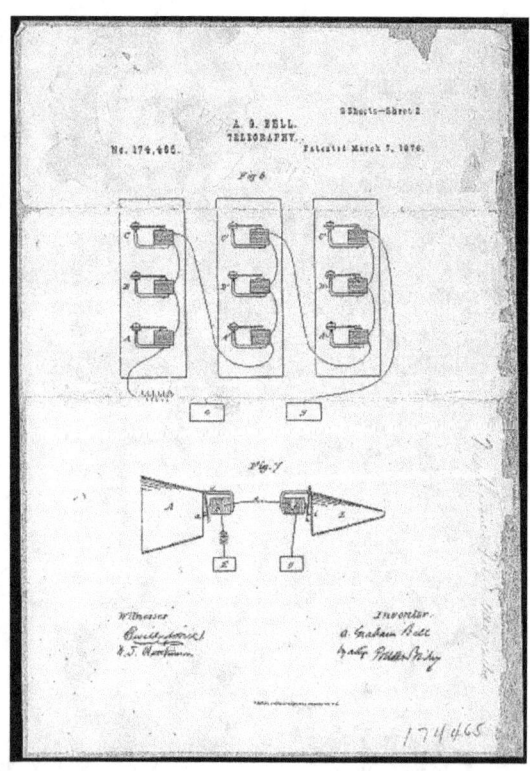

The first page of Bell's patent illustrations for his telephone. Public domain.

1876 – Alexander Graham Bell was granted patent #174,486 for an invention he called the telephone beating Antonio Meucci by four hours.

1916 - The manufacturing firms of Karl Rapp and Gustav Otto merged to form the Bayerische Flugzeugwerke AG (Bavarian Aircraft Works). The company would later become the Bayerische Motor-Werke (Bavarian Motor Works or BMW).

1923 - *The New Republic* became the first to publish Robert Frost's poem "Stopping By Woods on a Snowy Evening."

1933 - The first daytime radio serial ever, *Marie the Little French Princess*, debuted on CBS for a two year run.

1936 - Germany violated the Treaty of Versailles and the Locarno Pact by re-occupying the demilitarized zone of Rhineland.

1942 - The British evacuated Rangoon during WWII, having completed all essential demolition. The Japanese entered the city the next day.

1945 – The United States 9th Armored Division captured and crossed the Ludendorff Bridge over the Rhine at Remagen in Germany, which helped shorten WWII.

Ludendorff Bridge near Remagen, Germany in the early 20's. Public domain.

1951 - Iranian Prime Minister Ali Razmara was assassinated in a mosque in Tehran.

1955 - *Peter Pan*, starring Mary Martin and Cyril Richard, was first presented as a television special. It made its appearance on NBC-TV.

1955 - Phyllis Diller, the comedian, made her first appearance ever at the Purple Onion in San Francisco, California. Her engagement there lasted 87 consecutive weeks.

1955 - Baseball Commissioner Ford Frick said he was in favor of legalizing the spitball, saying, "It's a great pitch and one of the easiest to throw." As of this writing, this pitch was still illegal.

Police wait for marchers to come across the Edmund Pettus Bridge in Selma, Alabama. Public domain.

1965 – It was called Bloody Sunday: A group of 600 civil rights marchers were forcefully broken up in Selma, Alabama.

1985 – "We Are the World" was played on the radio around the world.

1986 – More than two months following the Space Shuttle *Challenger* explosion, Divers from the USS *Preserver* locate the crew cabin of Challenger on the Atlantic Ocean floor.

1988 - After rejecting what the Alliance of Motion Picture and Television Producers (AMPTP) said was a final offer, representatives of the Writers Guild of America (WGA) called a strike for all the union's members.

1989 - Iran broke off diplomatic relations with Britain over Salman Rushdie's novel, *Satanic Verses*.

1992 - Former Soviet Foreign Minister Eduard Shevardnadze returned to his native Georgia.

1992 - A new four-party coalition government, led by Jean-Luc Dehaene, was formed in Belgium.

1994 – The U.S. Supreme Court ruled that parodies of an original work are generally covered by the doctrine of fair use.

1996 - Three United States servicemen were jailed in Japan for up to seven years for the abduction and rape of an Okinawa schoolgirl a year earlier.

2007 – British House of Commons voted to make the upper chamber, the House of Lords, 100% elected.

MARCH 8th

BIRTHDAYS FOR MARCH 8th

1783 Hannah Van Buren; U.S. First Lady

1841 Oliver Wendell Holmes; Member of the Supreme Court of the U.S., writer

1921 Alan Hale, Jr.; American actor

1939 Jim Bouton; baseball, writer

1940 Sue Ane Langdon (Lookhoff); actress

1942 Dick Allen; baseball

1943 Lynn Redgrave; actress

1945 Mickey Dolenz; singer

1946 Randy Meisner; musician, bassist, singer

1947 Mike Allsup; musician, guitarist

1947 Carole Bayer Sager; singer, songwriter

1948 Little Peggy March (Margaret Annemarie Battavio); singer

1958 Gary Numan; singer

1959 Aidan Quinn; actor

1959 Lester Holt; American television journalist

1961 Camryn Manheim; actress

1964 Peter Gill; musician, drummer

1976 Freddie Prinze, Jr.; actor

1977 James Van Der Beek; actor

EVENTS FOR MARCH 8th

1669 - On the island of Sicily in modern-day Italy, Mount Etna began rumbling. Multiple eruptions over the next few weeks killed more than 20,000 people and left thousands homeless.

1702 – Anne Stuart, sister of Mary II, became Queen regnant of England, Scotland, and Ireland.

1817 – The New York Stock Exchange was founded.

1849 - Thomas Ewing of Ohio was appointed by President Zachary Taylor as the first Secretary of the Interior Department.

1887 – Everett Horton patented the telescopic fishing rod, made of one steel tube inside another.

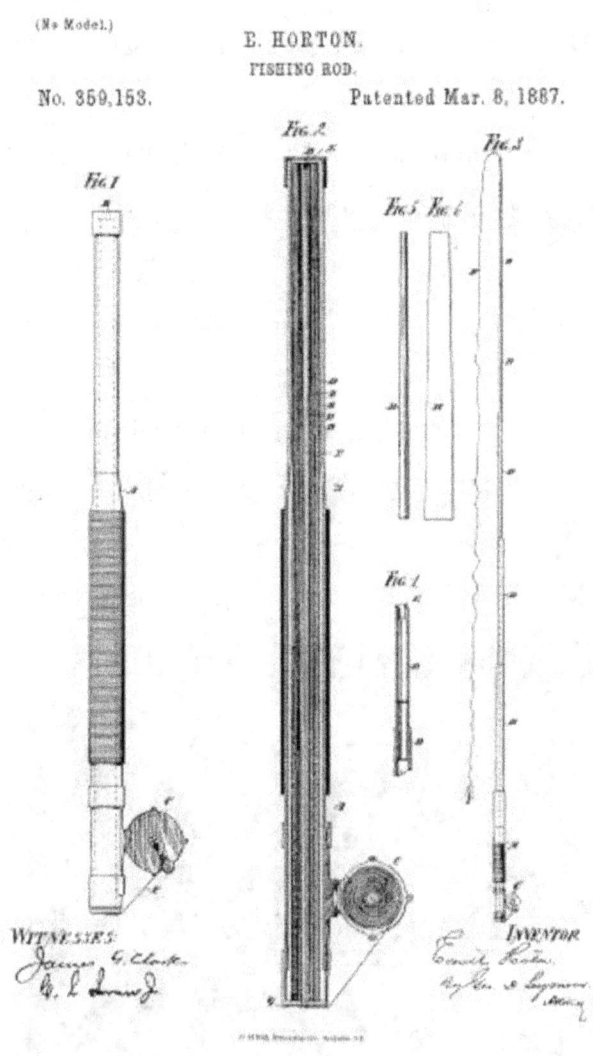

Patent drawing for Horton's fishing rod. Public domain.

1894 - In New York, a dog license law was enacted, marking the first such animal control law in the United States. The cost of the license was $2 per year.

1910 - The Royal Aero Club issued the first British pilot's license to J.T.C Moore Brabazon.

1917 - Riots and strikes in St. Petersburg marked the start of the "February Revolution" in Russia.

1920 - Denmark joined the League of Nations.

1921 - French troops occupied Duesseldorf and other towns in the Ruhr after Germany failed to pay reparations.

1936 – Daytona Beach Road Course held their first oval stock car race.

1948 - The United States Supreme Court ruled that religious instruction in public schools violated the constitution in the case of McCollum v. Board of Education.

1949 – Mildred Gillars ("Axis Sally"), female radio personality during World War II, best known for her propaganda broadcasts for Nazi Germany, was condemned to prison on one count of treason.

The Volkswagen bus. Photo by Erik Meltzer. Creative Commons License; used by permission.

1950 – Volkswagen began production of the Volkswagen Type 2, or better known as the Volkswagen bus.

Ward's Daily Almanac; The Book of March page 64

1954 - Herb McKenley set a world record for the quarter mile in Melbourne, Australia. He ran the distance in 46.8 seconds.

1957 - The courts ruled the International Boxing Club was a monopoly, and thus was in violation of the Sherman Anti-Trust Law.

1957 - Following Israel's withdrawal from occupied Egyptian territory, the Suez Canal was reopened to international traffic.

1962 - The Beatles gave their first broadcast performance on BBC Radio.

1963 – The Ba'ath Party came to power in Syria in a Coup d'état by a clique of quasi-leftist Syrian Army officers calling themselves the National Council of the Revolutionary Command.

1968 - Rock show promoter, Bill Graham of San Francisco, California moved to the East coast to open Fillmore East in New York City.

1969 - The Pontiac Firebird Trans Am was introduced at the Chicago Auto Show.

1971 – After fifteen rounds in a boxing match billed as "The Fight of the Century," "Smokin' Joe" Frazier won a decision over Muhammad Ali, previously undefeated, to become the world heavyweight boxing champion.

1973 - Former Beatle Paul McCartney was fined 100 pounds (about $240 U.S.) for growing marijuana on his and wife Linda's farm in Campbeltown, Scotland.

1974 – The Aéroport de Paris Nord (Paris North Airport) had been operating for 8 years. Today, they changed their name to the Charles de Gaulle Airport.

1975 - Olivia Newton-John reached #1 on the pop charts with "Have You Never Been Mellow."

1978 - Belgian millionaire Baron Charles Bracht was kidnapped. No ransom demands were ever made, and he was not known for having political enemies. His body was found on April 10.

1979 – Philips demonstrated the Compact Disc publicly for the first time.

1983 – President Ronald Reagan referred to the Soviet Union as an "evil empire" for the second time in his political career.

1985 – A failed assassination attempt on Sayyed Mohammad Hussein Fadlallah in Beirut, Lebanon, killed at least 45 and injured 175 others.

1993 – The animated program *Beavis and Butthead* began airing on MTV.

1994 – A commuter train that was traveling at an accelerated speed around a sharp turn derailed and fell into a gorge near Durban, South Africa; at least 88 persons were known dead, and more than 350 were injured in Natal province's worst railroad accident.

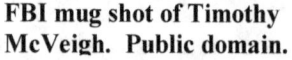

FBI mug shot of Timothy McVeigh. Public domain.

1996 - An updated remake of *La Cage Aux Folles, The Birdcage* starring Robin Williams, Nathan Lane, Gene Hackman, Dianne Wiest, and Calista Flockhart, opened in United States theaters.

1999 – The Supreme Court of the United States upheld the murder convictions of

Timothy McVeigh for the Oklahoma City bombing.

2004 – A new constitution was signed by Iraq's Governing Council.

MARCH 9th

BIRTHDAYS FOR MARCH 9th

1902 Will Geer (William Auge Ghere); actor

1918 Mickey Spillane; writer

1921 Carl Betz; actor

1923 James Buckley; politician

1933 Lloyd Price; songwriter, record label owner, producer

1934 Yuri Gagarin; Russian cosmonaut: the first man to travel in space

1934 Joyce Van Patten; actress

1936 Mickey Gilley; American musician and singer

1941 Jim Colbert; golf

1942 Mark Lindsay; saxophonist, singer, songwriter

1943 Bobby Fischer; World Chess Champion

1943 Charles Gibson; American television journalist

1943 Trish Van Devere; actress

1944 Trevor Burton; musician, guitarist

1945 Robin Trower; musician, guitarist

1946 Jim Cregan; musician, guitarist

1948 Jeffrey Osborne; musician, drummer, singer

1950 Andy North; golf

1951 Spencer Thomas; football

1957 Faith Daniels; American journalist

1958 Martin Fry; singer

1958 Linda Fiorentino; actress

1961 Rick Steiner (Robert Rechsteiner); American wrestler

1964 Steve Wilkos; American police officer and talk show host

1964 Juliette Binoche; actress

1965 Brian Bosworth; football

1965 Benito Santiago; baseball

1971 Emmanuel Lewis; actor

1979 Melina Perez; WWE Diva

EVENTS FOR MARCH 9*th*

1500 – The fleet of Pedro Alvares Cabral departed Lisbon for the Indies on a journey which would lead to the discovery of Brazil.

1796 - Napoleon Bonaparte married his first wife Josephine de Beauharnais.

1799 - United States Congress contracted Simeon North, of Berlin, Connecticut, to make 500 horse pistols that cost the government $6.50 each.

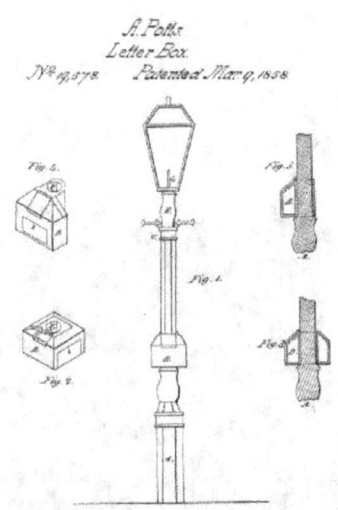

1856 – The national fraternity Sigma Alpha Epsilon was founded at the University of Alabama in Tuscaloosa, Alabama.

1858 – Albert Potts, of Philadelphia opened his mailbox to find he had

Patent drawing for Albert Potts' mailbox. Public domain.

been awarded a patent for the mailbox. (Specifically, he patented a method for attaching a mailbox to a street lamp. Why? We may never know.)

1859 - The National Association of Baseball Players adopted a rule limiting the size of bats to less than 2 ½ inches in diameter.

1862 – During the American Civil War, the USS Monitor and CSS Virginia fought to a draw in the Battle of Hampton Roads, the first battle between two ironclad warships.

1864 - General Ulysses S. Grant was appointed Lieutenant General of the Union armies during the American Civil War. Before him, only George Washington had held that rank.

1916 – Pancho Villa led nearly 500 Mexican raiders in an attack against Columbus, New Mexico.

Ruins of Columbus, New Mexico after being raided by Pancho Villa. Pubic domain.

1933 – Reacting to the Great Depression, President Franklin D. Roosevelt submitted the Emergency Banking Act to Congress, the first of his New Deal policies.

1938 - Comedian Bob Hope made his film debut, singing "Thanks for the Memories" in *The Big Broadcast of 1938*.

1949 - The first all-electric dining car was placed into service on the Illinois Central Railroad.

1954 – CBS television aired the *See It Now* episode, "A Report on Senator Joseph McCarthy," produced by Fred Friendly and Edward R. Murrow.

1954 - WNBT-TV, now WNBC-TV, New York, broadcast the first local color television commercials. Reportedly, the commercial was for a company called Castro Decorators, Inc.

1955 - The film version of John Steinbeck's novel, *East of Eden*, starring James Dean and Julie Harris, premiered in New York City.

1959 - Jack Paar appeared on the cover of *LIFE* magazine.

1959 – The Barbie doll made its debut at the American International Toy Fair in New York.

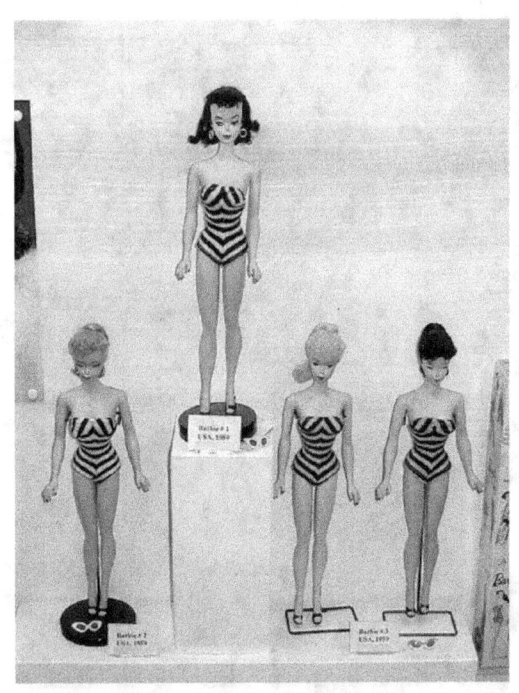

The original Barbie Doll collection as it appeared in 1959. Creative Commons License; used by permission.

1967 – Trans World Airlines Flight 553, a Douglas DC-9-15, crashed in a field in Concord Township, Ohio following a mid-air collision with a Beechcraft Baron, killing 26.

1976 – Forty-two people died in Cavalese, Italy in the world's worst cable car disaster to date; one teen-age girl survived.

1977 – In a 39-hour standoff, armed Hanafi Muslims seized three Washington, D.C. buildings, killed two people, and took 149 hostages. The buildings they took were the District Building (now called the John A. Wilson Building), B'nai B'rith headquarters, and the Islamic Center of Washington.

1987 - Chrysler Corporation made an offer to buy American Motors Corporation for up to $1 billion dollars.

1989 – A worker's strike forced Eastern Air Lines into bankruptcy.

**Official portrait of Dr. Antonia Novello.
Public domain.**

1990 – Dr. Antonia Novello was sworn in as Surgeon General of the United States, becoming the first female and Hispanic American to serve in that position.

1991 - Yugoslavia deployed tanks in Belgrade after bloody clashes between riot police and tens of thousands of anti-Communist protesters.

1993 – Rodney King testified

against the four LAPD officers accused of violating his civil rights when they beat him during his 1991 arrest.

1994 - Five Irish Republican Army mortar bombs landed on the runway at London's Heathrow airport but failed to explode.

1995 – Ignoring opposition from the British Government, President Bill Clinton approved a visa for Irish nationalist leader Gerry Adams to enter the United States.

1996 – George Burns died peacefully at his Beverly Hills home at the age of 100.

1997 – Observers in China, Mongolia and eastern Siberia were treated to a rare double feature as an eclipse permitted the Hale-Bopp Comet to be seen during the day.

George Burns at age 90. Picture by Allan Warren. Creative Commons License; used by permission.

MARCH 10th

BIRTHDAYS FOR MARCH 10th

1916 Pamela Mason (Ostrer); writer, actress

1920 Jethro (Kenneth Burns); entertainer, musician, mandolin and banjo player

1923 Don Abney; jazz pianist, studio musician

1928 James Earl Ray; assassin

1940 Chuck Norris; karate champion, actor

1947 Kim Campbell; 19th prime minister of Canada

1957 Shannon Tweed; actress

1957 Osama bin Laden; Islamist and leader of al-Qaeda

1958 Sharon Stone; actress

1961 Mitch Gaylord; American gymnast

1964 Neneh Cherry (Nenah Mariann Karlsson); songwriter, rap singer

1964 Prince Edward; Earl of Wessex

1964 Jasmine Guy; actress

1966 Edie Brickell; folksinger

1977 Shannon Miller; gymnast

1983 Carrie Underwood; American country singer

EVENTS FOR MARCH 10th

1528 – Balthasar Hubmaier, one of the foremost leaders of the Austrian Anabaptists, was burned at the stake as a heretic in Vienna.

1804 – In St. Louis, Missouri a formal ceremony was conducted to transfer ownership of the Louisiana Territory from France to the United States.

Depiction of German Anabaptist Balthasar by Christoffel van Sichem. Public domain.

1849 - Abraham Lincoln applied for a patent on a device to lift vessels over shoals (sandbars) using inflated cylinders.

1863 – Prince Albert Edward (later King Edward VII) of England married Princess Alexandra of Denmark.

1876 – Only three days after his patent was issued, Alexander Graham Bell sent the first clear telephone message, to a nearby room, telling his assistant, Mr. Watson, "Mr. Watson, come here, I want you."

1891 – Almon Strowger, an undertaker in Topeka, Kansas, patented the "Strowger Switch," a device which led to the automation of telephone circuit switching.

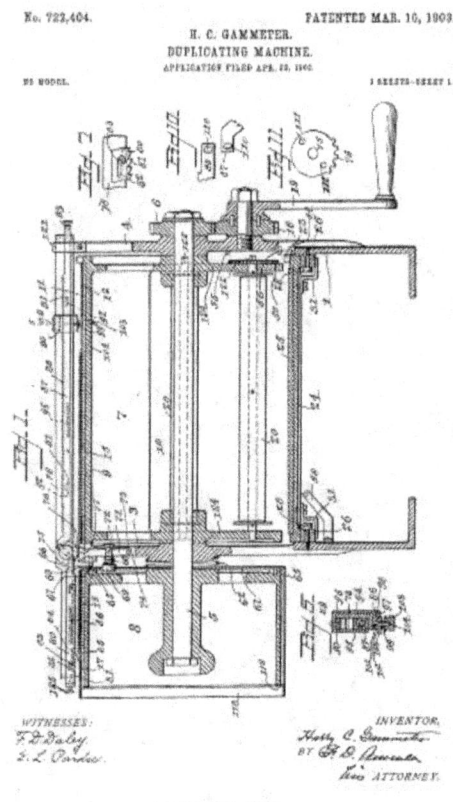

One of the patent drawings for Harry Gammeter's duplicating machine. Public domain.

1903 – Cleveland, Ohio's Harry C. Gammeter patented the multigraph duplicating machine, a forerunner of the office copier.

1906 - An underground fire sparked a massive explosion that virtually destroyed a vast maze of mines and killed over 1,000 workers in Courrieres, France.

1912 - Yuan Shi-kai was installed as the provisional president of the Republic of China.

1913 - William Knox rolled the first perfect 300-game in tournament competition at the American Bowling Congress tournament held in Toledo, Ohio.

1918 - Warner Brothers released its first bona fide hit movie, *Four Years in Germany*.

1922 – Mahatma Gandhi was arrested in India, tried for sedition, and sentenced to six years in prison, only to be released after nearly two years for an appendicitis operation.

1922 - *Variety* magazine headline read, "Radio Sweeping Country - 1,000,000 sets in use."

1926 - The first Book-of-the-Month Club selection was published by Viking Press. The honor of being first went to *Lolly Willowes, or The Loving Huntsman* by English novelist Sylvia Townsend Warner.

1933 – An earthquake measuring 6.4 in Long Beach, California killed 115 people and caused an estimated $40 million dollars in damage.

1937 - An audience of 21,000 jitterbuggers crowded the Paramount Theatre in New York City to see the "King of Swing," Benny Goodman.

1939 – *The Little Princess*, starring Shirley Temple and based on Frances Hodgson Burnett's novel, opened in United States theaters.

Screenshot from *The Little Princess* starring Shirley Temple and Richard Greene. Public domain.

1941 - The Brooklyn Dodgers announced their players would be wearing batting helmets for the 1941 season.

1945 – Three hundred United States B-29 bombers devastated Japan's capital in what became known as the Great Tokyo Air Raid in World War II.

1949 - Louisa May Alcott's popular novel, *Little Women*, was again adapted for the screen, and opened in movie theaters.

1952 - The government of Cuba was overthrown by former president Fulgencio Batista, who ruled as a dictator until 1959.

1956 - Twenty-three year old Julie Andrews made her television debut when she appeared in the musical adaptation of Maxwell Anderson's play, *High Tor*. This was presented as a 90-minute episode of CBS Television's *Ford Star Jubilee*.

1965 - Walter Matthau and Art Carney opened in one of Neil Simon's greatest theatrical triumphs, *The Odd Couple*. The show ran for about 18 months.

James Earl Ray's mug shot. Public domain.

1966 - Anti-German protests marred the wedding of Princess Beatrix of the Netherlands to Claus von Amsberg, a West German diplomat, in Amsterdam.

1969 – James Earl Ray was sentenced in Memphis, Tennessee, to 99 years in prison for the murder of Martin Luther King Jr. in April 1968. Coincidentally, this was also Ray's birthday.

1970 - The U.S. Army accused Capt. Ernest Medina and four other soldiers of committing crimes at My Lai in March 1968. All eventually had their charges dismissed or were acquitted by courts-martial.

1972 - Marshal Lon Nol took over as Cambodian head of state.

1973 - The Governor of Bermuda, Sir Richard Sharples, was assassinated in the grounds of Government House.

1977 – Saturn was relegated to share the heavens with another ringed planet when 3 astronomers discovered rings around Uranus.

1980 – Madeira School headmistress Jean Harris shot and killed her lover Doctor Herman Tarnower, author of *The Complete Scarsdale Medical Diet.*

1990 - Haitian President Prosper Avril resigned 18 months after seizing power in a coup.

1992 - NATO and its former Soviet enemies pledged that a treaty slashing conventional forces in Europe would be put into effect within four months.

1993 – President Suharto of Indonesia was re-elected for a seventh five-year term of office despite his previous announcement that he did not intend to run again.

President Suharto at the beginning of his 6th term. Public domain.

1996 - Five Latin American presidents approved the creation of an Andean Community economic bloc to replace the Andean Pact trade group which was called the Trujillo Protocol.

1997 - The fledgling Warner Brothers (WB) television network airs the first episode of what would become its first bona-fide hit show, *Buffy the Vampire Slayer*.

2000 – The NASDAQ Composite stock market index peaked at 5132.52, signaling the beginning of the end of the dot-com boom.

2006 – The Mars Reconnaissance Orbiter, a NASA multipurpose spacecraft designed to conduct reconnaissance and exploration of Mars from orbit, achieved a Martian orbit.

Mars Reconnaissance Orbiter over Mars (conceptual drawing). Public domain.

MARCH 11th

BIRTHDAYS FOR MARCH 11th

1731 Robert Treat Paine; jurist, signer of the US Declaration of Independence

1885 Malcolm Campbell; auto racer, 1st to drive more than 300 mph in a car

1903 Lawrence Welk; bandleader

1915 J. C. R. Licklider; American computer scientist and Internet pioneer

1916 Harold Wilson; British Prime Minister

1919 Mercer Ellington; bandleader, songwriter

1930 Troy Ruttman; auto racer

1931 Rupert Murdoch; newspaper publisher

1934 Sam Donaldson; newsman

1935 Nancy Kovack; actress

1936 Antonin Scalia; U.S. Supreme Court Justice

1948 Roy Barnes; Governor of Georgia

1950 Windlan Hall; football

1950 Jerry Zucker; writer

1950 Bobby McFerrin; pianist, jazz musician, songwriter, singer

1952 Susan Richardson; actress

1956 Curtis Brown, Jr.; astronaut

1956 Joey Buttafuoco; American statutory rapist

1959 Nina Hartley; American porn star

1965 Jesse Jackson, Jr.; American politician

1968 Lisa Loeb; singer

1971 Johnny Knoxville; American television personality

EVENTS FOR MARCH 11th

1702 – The first English daily newspaper to meet with some success, *The Daily Courant*, was launched near Fleet Street in London.

1791 - Samuel Mulliken, of Philadelphia, Pennsylvania, became the first person to have more than one United States patent.   He received patents for a machine for threshing grain and corn, a machine for breaking and swingling hemp, a machine for cutting and polishing marble, and a machine for raising a nap on cloths.

1818 - *Frankenstein or, The Modern Prometheus* was published for the first time.

1824 – The United States War Department created the Bureau of Indian Affairs.

1845 - Unhappy with translational differences regarding the Treaty of Waitangi, chiefs Hone Heke, Kawiti and Māori tribe members chopped down the British flagpole for a fourth time and drove settlers out of Kororareka, New Zealand during the Flagstaff War.

1851 - The first performance of Giuseppe Verdi's opera *Rigoletto* was given in Venice.

1861 – The Constitution of the Confederate States of America was adopted by the southern states.

1864 – The largest man-made disaster ever to befall England to date killed over 250 people in Sheffield during the Great Sheffield Flood.

The Brooklyn Bridge during the Great Blizzard of '88. Public domain

1888 – A blizzard started along the Atlantic Seaboard, closing communication and transportation lines. The snow continued to fall for three days in the "Great Blizzard of '88."

1917 - General Stanley Maude, along with 50,000 British and Indian troops, marched into Baghdad, capturing 9,000 Turkish prisoners.

1927 - Samuel "Roxy" Rothafel opened the Roxy Theatre in New York City, which cost $12,000,000 to build and had 5,920 seats.

1927 - The Flatheads Gang committed the first armored-car robbery near Pittsburgh, Pennsylvania. It was reported that $104,000 was stolen.

William Taft's headstone in Arlington Cemetery. Public domain.

1930 – William Howard Taft became the first United States President to be buried in the National Cemetery in Arlington, Virginia.

1941 - President Franklin D. Roosevelt signed the "Lend-Lease Bill," which enabled Britain to borrow money to buy additional food and arms during World War II.

1945 – The Imperial Japanese Navy attempted a large-scale kamikaze attack on the U.S. Pacific Fleet anchored at Ulithi atoll in "Operation Tan No. 2."

1956 - Sir Lawrence Olivier starred in *Richard III* in a three-hour afternoon NBC-TV special. The network paid $500,000 for the rights to the program. This was the first time that a movie was released on television and in the theaters on the same day.

1958 - American League batters were required to wear batting helmets.

1960 – Pioneer 5 was launched into orbit around the sun.

Pioneer 5. Photo courtesy of NASA.

1964 - Raul Leoni received the title of "Senator for Life" of Venezuela.

1967 - Jean-Claude Killy of France won the World Cup skiing title.

1970 – Writer Erle Stanley Gardner died at age 80 in Temecula, California.

1973 - Hector J. Campora won the first presidential election to be held in Argentina in ten years.

Erle Stanley Gardner, the author of Perry Mason mysteries and many other books. Photo by John Atherton. Creative Commons License; used by permission.

1981 - Chilean President Augusto Pinochet who had assumed his office through a coup d'état 16 years earlier, was replaced as President of the Junta by Admiral Merino.

1985 - Mikhail Gorbachev became head of the Soviet Union following the death of Konstantin Chernenko. At 54, he was the youngest member of the ruling Politburo.

1985 - The Egyptian Al-Fayed brothers won control of the retailer House of Fraser in London and thus gained control of the department store Harrods.

The twin-stick Popsicle. Public domain.

1986 – Popsicle announced plans to cease producing the traditional twin-stick frozen treat for a one-stick model.

1988 - French authorities dug up the remains of legendary French singer and actor Yves Montand and took them to a laboratory for DNA tests to settle a paternity suit. A woman claimed that he had fathered her daughter, but the DNA test proved otherwise.

1989 - *COPS*, a documentary-style television series that follows police officers and sheriff's deputies as they go about their jobs, debuted on Fox.

1997 – Former Beatles member Paul McCartney was knighted by Queen Elizabeth II for his "services to music."

1999 – Infosys became the first company from India to be listed on the NASDAQ stock exchange.

2004 – Simultaneous explosions on rush hour trains in Madrid, Spain killed 191 people.

2005 – Brian Nichols went on a shooting rampage at the Fulton County courthouse in Atlanta, Georgia, killing three. He killed a fourth person before surrendering to the police the next day.

2006 – Michelle Bachelet was inaugurated as first female president of Chile.

2009 - The Toyota Motor Company announced that it had sold over 1 million gas-electric hybrid vehicles in the U.S. under its six Toyota and Lexus brands.

MARCH 12th

BIRTHDAYS FOR MARCH 12th

1806 Jane Pierce; U.S. First Lady

1832 Charles Boycott; real estate agent and source of the term "to boycott."

1914 Julia Lennon; John Lennon's mother

1921 Gordon MacRae; actor

1923 Wally Shirra, Jr.; astronaut

1923 Mae Young; American professional wrestler

1926 George Ariyoshi; Governor of Hawaii

1931 Herbert Kelleher; Southwest Airlines co-founder

1932 Andrew Young; U.S. Ambassador to the United Nations, Mayor of Atlanta, GA

1932 Barbara Feldon; American actress and model

1936 Eddie Sutton; College basketball coach

1938 Johnny Rutherford; auto racer: Indianapolis 500 winner

1938 Lew Dewitt; singer

1940 Al Jarreau; singer, songwriter

1946 Liza Minnelli; American singer and actress

1947 Mitt Romney; former Governor of Massachusetts, 2008 Presidential Candidate

1948 James Taylor; musician, singer

1948 Kent Conrad; U.S. Senator

1953 Ron Jeremy; American pornographic actor

1957 Marlon Jackson; singer

1962 Darryl Eugene Strawberry; baseball

EVENTS FOR MARCH 12th

1470 - Edward IV defeated the rebels at the battle of Empingham in the "Wars of the Roses."

1664 – New Jersey became a colony of England.

1884 - The State of Mississippi authorized the first state-supported college for women in the United States at the Mississippi Industrial Institute and College (now known as the Mississippi University for Women).

1889 - Almon B. Strowger filed for a patent for his invention, the automatic telephone system. It worked, but not well enough, and Mr. Bell's was deemed more reliable. Still, the patent was granted two years later.

1894 – Coca-Cola was sold in bottles for the first time. The first bottling took place in Vicksburg, Mississippi.

1907 - At Toulon, France, the battleship *Iena* exploded in dry-dock and killed at least 118 men.

1912 – Juliette Low founded the Girl Scouts of the U.S.A.

Juliet Low (center), founder of the Girl Scouts. Public domain.

1913 - Canberra became the capital of Australia when the foundation stone of the Federal Parliament building was laid.

1918 – Moscow became the capital of Russia . . . again. Saint Petersburg had held this status for 215 years.

1928 – The St. Francis Dam collapsed in California, killing over 600 people.

1930 - Mahatma Gandhi began a 300-mile protest journey in India to defy a British law establishing a monopoly in producing salt.

Roosevelt shortly after one of his "fireside chats."
Public domain.

1933 – Franklin D. Roosevelt addressed the nation for the first time as President of the United States. This was also the first of his "fireside chats."

1938 - One day after Artur Seyss-Inquart became Chancellor of Austria, German troops invaded the country.

1940 - Finland signed a peace treaty with the Soviet Union, ending the 14-week war which the Russians won by sheer weight of numbers.

1964 – New Hampshire became the first state to legally sell lottery tickets in the 20th century.

1966 - The Indonesian Congress stripped Dr. Sukarno of all powers including the title of president. General Suharto became acting president until general elections in 1968.

1966 - Bobby Hull, of the Chicago Blackhawks, became the first National Hockey League player to score 51 points in one season.

Paul McCartney in performance with his wife Linda. Photo by Jim Summaria. Creative commons License; used by permission.

1969 – Paul McCartney married photographer Linda Eastman. And while Paul and Linda were exchanging their vows (see next entry) . . .

1969 - The London home of George and Pattie Harrison was raided and a large amount of marijuana was confiscated.

1971 - The March 12 Memorandum was sent to the Demirel government of Turkey and the government resigns.

1973 - In Syria, a new and permanent constitution was endorsed by over 97 percent of voters in a national referendum.

1974 - *Wonder Woman* debuted on ABC-TV and eventually moved to CBS.

1979 - Prime Minister Sir Eric Gairy and his government in Grenada were overthrown and replaced by Maurice Bishop of the New Jewel Movement.

1981 - Two Soviet cosmonauts, Vladimir Kovalyonok and Viktor Savinykh, were launched into space and headed to the *Salyut 6* space station for a 75-day mission to the facility, which had been in orbit since 1977.

1984 – More than 187,000 miners walked off the job all across Britain in a strike that lasted one week shy of a full year.

1987 - Both Coca-Cola and Boeing Company joined Dow Jones Industrials, replacing Owens-Illinoise and Inco, respectively.

Portrait of "Cosette" by Emile Bayard, from the original edition of Les Misérables (1862). This image is still used for the production. Public domain.

1987 – After breaking all records for advance ticket sales, the British musical Les Miserables opened on Broadway. The show ran until May of 2003, with more than 6,600 performances. It would open again three years later.

1988 - A sudden hailstorm prompted fans at a soccer match in Katmandu, Nepal to flee. Fearing injury from Mother Nature, the fans began to rush to seek cover, and the resulting stampede killed at least 70 people and injured hundreds more.

1992 - The Indian Ocean island

of Mauritius became a republic dropping its links with the British crown 24 years to the day after independence.

1993 - Nearly 250 people were killed and more than 700 were injured when up to 13 bombs went off across the city of Bombay in India.

1993 – After having been confirmed the previous day by the U.S. Senate, Janet Reno was sworn in as the first female attorney general of the United States.

Official portrait of Janet Reno. Public domain.

1993 – Snow began to fall across the eastern portion of the US with tornadoes, thunder snowstorms, high winds and record low temperatures. The storm lasted for 30 hours and has since been referred to as "The Blizzard of 1993."

1994 - The Church of England broke with 460 years of male dominance when it ordained its first women priests in Bristol Cathedral.

1996 - China began new war games in the Taiwan Strait in a show of force, using jets and warships to drive home its warning to Taiwan not to seek independence.

2003 - Fifteen-year old Elizabeth Smart was found in Sandy, Utah, nine months after being abducted from her family's home. David Mitchell and Wanda Barzee were charged with kidnapping, burglary and sexual assault.

2003 - After having performed a London concert two nights earlier, the country group, the Dixie Chicks, began receiving backlash from an anti-Bush statement they had made during their show. The statement had come at a time when President Bush's approval rating was still high prior to the beginning of the Iraq War and the statement, which had been quoted in *The Guardian*, incited millions of people to call radio stations asking them to remove the country band from air-play.

2004 – President of South Korea, Roh Moo-hyun, was impeached by its national assembly for the first time in the nation's history.

2005 – Tung Chee Hwa, the first Chief Executive of Hong Kong, stepped down from his post after his resignation was approved by the Chinese central government.

MARCH 13th

BIRTHDAYS FOR MARCH 13th

1733 Joseph Priestley; chemist, discovered oxygen

1798 Abigail Fillmore; U.S. First Lady

1855 Percival Lowell; astronomer

1908 Walter Annenberg; publisher, philanthropist

1910 Sammy Kaye; bandleader

1911 L. Ron Hubbard; religious founder, author

1914 Edward O'Hare; American pilot, namesake of O'Hare International Airport.

1919 Eddie Pellagrini; baseball

1921 Al Jaffee; American cartoonist

1932 Jan Howard; country singer

1933 Mike Stoller; American songwriter

1939 Neil Sedaka; songwriter, singer

1950 William H. Macy; actor

1951 Steve Craig; football

1953 Andy Bean; golf

1953 Deborah Raffin; actress

1956 Dana Delany; actress

1959 Kathy Hilton; socialite-Hilton Hotels, mother of Nicky Hilton and Paris Hilton

1963 Vance Edward Johnson; football

1987 Marco Andretti; American racecar driver (grandson of Mario Andretti, son of Michael Andretti)

EVENTS FOR MARCH 13th

1639 – Harvard College was named for clergyman John Harvard.

1781 – William Herschel discovered the 7th planet in our solar system: Uranus.

1791 – Thomas Paine's *The Rights of Man* was published in London.

1809 - King Gustavus IV of Sweden was overthrown in a coup d'etat and was succeeded by his uncle Charles XIII.

Title page from *The Rights of Man*. Public domain.

1813 - Sweden joined the Grand Alliance against Napoleon and his allies.

1848 - After demonstrations and riots in Vienna, Prince Metternich resigned as chancellor.

1858 - Felice Orsini, Italian revolutionary, was executed by guillotine for his part in the assassination attempt on Napoleon III of France.

1862 – The U.S. federal government prohibited all Union army officers from returning fugitive slaves, thus effectively annulling the "Fugitive Slave Law of 1850" and set the stage for the Emancipation Proclamation.

1865 - During the U.S. Civil War, the Confederate Congress under President Jefferson Davis allowed slaves to join the army in exchange for freedom.

1877 – Chester Greenwood, of Farmington, Maine, patented the earmuff.

1881 - Czar Alexander II of Russia, died after a bomb was thrown at him near the Winter Palace.

1897 – San Diego State University was founded as San Diego Normal School.

1900 - The British under Lord Frederick Roberts captured Bloemfontein in the Boer War.

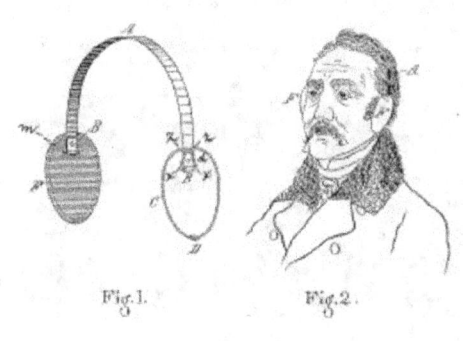

Original patent drawings for the earmuff.
Public domain.

1901 - Benjamin Harrison,

the 23rd president of the United States, died; he was the only president to date to succeed and be succeeded by the same man: Grover Cleveland.

1930 - The discovery of the planet Pluto was announced. It was discovered a month earlier by Clyde Tombaugh.

1938 - Léon Blum became prime minister of France and formed the Popular Front ministry.

1940 - Hostilities between Russia and Finland in what was called "The Winter War" ceased at noon.

Sheet music cover for "Wait 'Til the Sun Shines, Nellie" as it was published in 1905. Public domain.

1942 – Bing Crosby and Mary Martin recorded "Wait Till the Sun Shines, Nellie."

1943 – German forces liquidated the Jewish ghetto in Kraków. Hans Finke arrived in Auschwitz with 963 other prisoners. Almost 500 were put to death in the gas chambers. The remaining prisoners were assigned to slave labor.

1947 - The musical *Brigadoon* opened for the first time at New York's Ziegfeld Theatre where it would run for 581 performances.

1947 - For the first time, the Academy Awards ceremony was opened to the general public. On that night the award for Best Picture went to *The Best Years of Our Lives*.

1969 - The Walt Disney studio released *The Love Bug*. Directed by Robert Stevenson, the film starred "Herbie," a lovable Volkswagen bug with a personality.

1969 – After testing the Lunar Module, *Apollo 9* returned safely to Earth.

The prime crew of *Apollo 9*. From left to right, James A. McDivitt (CMDR), David R. Scott (CMP) and Russell L. Schweickart (LMP). Public domain.

1970 - An extremely popular cover of *LIFE* magazine was issued, showing the current fashion battle over long versus mini skirts.

1972 - Clifford Irving admitted to a New York court that he had fabricated his autobiography of Howard Hughes and defrauded his publisher McGraw Hill.

1972 - Britain and China resumed full diplomatic relations after 22 years; Britain withdrew its consulate from Taiwan.

1990 - The Soviet parliament voted to end the seven-decade political monopoly of the Communist Party.

1991 – The United States Department of Justice announced that Exxon agreed to pay $1 billion for the clean up of the Exxon Valdez oil spill in Alaska.

1992 - It was reported in *USA Today* that Tammy Faye Bakker filed for divorce from her husband, Jim Bakker, who was in prison for his fraudulent dealings with the PTL ministry.

1992 – An earthquake registering 6.8 on the Richter scale killed over 500 in Erzincan, eastern Turkey.

1996 - A man with four guns shot and killed 16 children and a teacher in a school in Dunblane, Scotland. He then shot himself. The man was identified as Thomas Watt Hamilton, a former Scout leader. Although the theorics flourish, the motive he had for this killing remains a mystery.

1997 - A Jordanian soldier shot and killed seven Israeli girls on a school trip to the Jordan River island of Naharayim, known as the Island of Peace, on the Israeli-Jordanian border. Witnesses said a bus dropped off about 40 girls at the observation post. While the girls admired the view, there was a hail of automatic gunfire as the soldier, Lance Cpl. Ahmed Yousef Mustafa, chased the terrified seventh and eighth graders down a hill. He had changed ammunition clips before other Jordanian soldiers overpowered him.

1997 - Sister Nirmala was elected as the new Superior-General of the Missionaries of Charity, succeeding Mother Teresa.

1997 – The Phoenix lights were seen over Phoenix, Arizona by hundreds of people, and by millions on television. There were two events involved in the incident: a triangular formation of lights seen to pass over the state, and a series of stationary lights seen in the Phoenix area. Military flares dropped from aircraft, was just one of the explanations provided for the phenomenon.

2003 – The journal *Nature* reported that 350,000-year-old footprints of an upright-walking human had been found in Italy.

2005 – Terry Ratzmann shot and killed six members of the Living Church of God and the minister at the Sheraton Inn in Brookfield, Wisconsin before killing himself.

2008 – Gold prices on the New York Mercantile Exchange hit $1,000 per ounce for the first time.

MARCH 14th

BIRTHDAYS FOR MARCH 14th

1863 Casey Jones; railroad engineer

1879 Albert Einstein; Nobel Prize-winning physicist

1912 Les Brown; bandleader

1914 Lee Petty; American race car driver

1918 Dennis Patrick; actor

1920 Hank Ketcham; cartoonist

1921 S. Truett Cathy; founder of Chick-fil-A

1925 William Clay Ford, Sr.; American owner of the Detroit Lions, grandson of Henry Ford

1928 Frank Borman; NASA astronaut

1933 Michael Caine (Maurice Joseph Micklewhite); Academy Award-winning actor

1933 Quincy Jones; composer, bandleader, record producer

1934 Eugene Cernan; astronaut

1934 Shirley Scott; musician, blues-oriented organist

1948 Tom Coburn; Senator from Oklahoma

1948 Billy Crystal; actor, comedian, writer

1950 Michael Gerald Ford; son of U.S. President Gerald R. Ford

1950 Rick Dees; disc jockey, comedian

1960 Kirby Puckett; baseball

1979 Santino Marella (Anthony Carelli); American professional wrestler

1983 Taylor Hanson; singer

EVENTS FOR MARCH 14*th*

1489 - Catherine Cornaro, Queen of Cyprus and last of the Lusignan dynasty, sold her kingdom to Venice.

1647 - In the Thirty Years War, a Treaty of Neutrality was signed at Ulm between France, Sweden, Bavaria and Cologne.

1757 - British Admiral John Byng was executed by firing squad for his bungled attempt to relieve the island of Minorca threatened by the French fleet.

1794 – Eli Whitney patented the cotton gin.

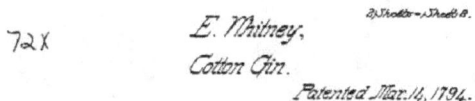

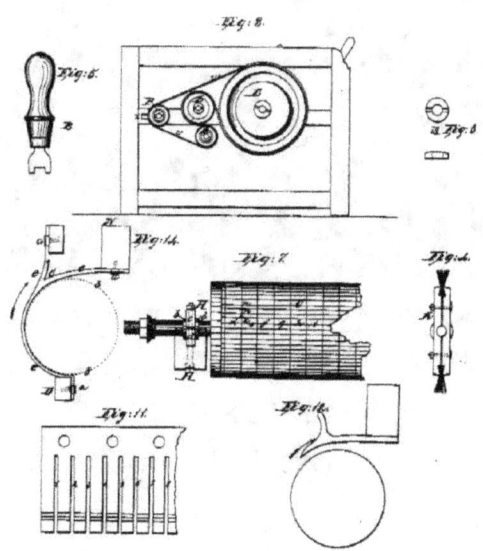

1864 - Samuel Baker discovered another source of the Nile in East Africa and named it Lake Albert Nyanza.

1885 - *The Mikado*, the comic operetta by Gilbert and Sullivan, premiered at the Savoy Theatre, London.

1900 – The Gold Standard Act was ratified, and placed United States currency on the gold standard.

Patent drawing for Eli Whitney's cotton gin. Public domain.

1910 - The "Lakeview Gusher Number One" was an immense out-of-control gushing oil well in the Midway-Sunset Oil Field in Kern County, California, resulting in what is regarded as one of the largest oil spills to date. The gusher began on this date and lasted 8 months. All in all, 9 million barrels of crude oil was spilled.

1915 – In World War I, the German cruiser *Dresden* was sunk by the Royal Navy in the Pacific.

The German cruiser *Dresden* passing through the Kiel Canal. Public domain.

1918 - The first seagoing ship made of concrete was launched sideways at Redwood City, California. The ship, *Faith*, didn't sink, but it did cost $750,000 to build.

1922 - John "Jack" Mack, who co-founded what would become one of North America's largest makers of heavy-duty trucks, was killed when his car collided with a trolley in Pennsylvania.

1923 - United States President Warren G. Harding became the first Chief Executive to file a tax return.

1932 - George Eastman, American photographic pioneer who founded the company Kodak, committed suicide. He shot himself once through the heart and left a suicide note which read, "My work is done. Why wait?"

1936 – The United States government went into the magazine business with *The Federal Register*. *The Register* is the official journal of the Federal Government of the United States that contains most routine publications and public notices of government agencies. It is a daily (except holidays) publication.

Cover of a contemporary edition of *The Federal Register*. Public domain.

1937 - In a publicity gag, Fred Allen and Jack Benny met on radio for "The Battle of the Century" on the *Jello Show*.

1939 - Hungary occupied the Carpatho-Ukraine and Slovakia declared its independence.

1942 – Orvan Hess and John Bumstead became the first doctors in the world to successfully treat a patient (Anne Miller) using penicillin.

1943 – During World War II the Kraków Ghetto was "liquidated;" the systematic deportation of all Jews. Eight thousand Jews deemed able to work were transported to the Plaszow labor camp. Those deemed unfit for work, some 2,000 Jews, were killed in the streets of the ghetto. Anyone remaining was sent to Auschwitz.

Columns of Jews carrying bundles march down a main street in Krakow during the liquidation of the ghetto. SS guards oversee the deportation action. Public domain.

1950 - The Federal Bureau of Investigation instituted the "Ten Most Wanted Fugitives" list in an effort to publicize particularly dangerous fugitives. The schmuck holding the very first #1 position was murderer/bank robber, Thomas James Holden.

1954 - The Vietnamese took the Gabrielle strongpoint against the French in the battle of Dien Bien Phu.

1958 - Perry Como was awarded the Recording Industry Association of America's (RIAA) first gold record, for "Catch a Falling Star."

1964 – Jack Ruby was found guilty of the murder of Lee Harvey Oswald, the accused assassin of United States President John F. Kennedy. He was sentenced to die in the electric chair, but he died of cancer while waiting for a new trial that he had won on appeal.

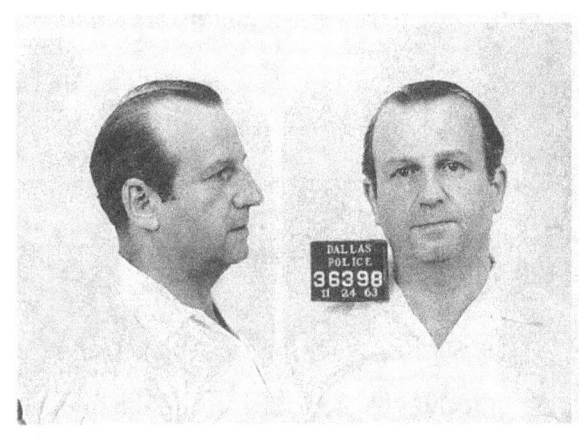

Jack Ruby's mug shot. Public domain.

1967 – The body of President John F. Kennedy was moved to a permanent burial place just a few feet away from the spot of his original internment at Arlington National Cemetery.

1976 - Egypt formally abrogated the 1971 Treaty of Friendship and Cooperation with the Soviet Union. The abrogation was announced in a speech by Anwar El Sedat which lasted more than three hours.

1978 - Dutch marines succeeded in freeing 71 hostages held by South Moluccans for 29 hours. Later on that same year, the South Moluccans were jailed for 15 years.

1979 - At least 200 people died when a Hawker Siddeley Trident aircraft crashed into a factory outside Peking, China. The crash was caused by an unqualified pilot who stole and flew the airliner.

1980 – Eighty-seven people, including a 14-man United States boxing team, died in an air crash in Warsaw.

1983 - OPEC agreed to cut its oil prices by 15 percent for the first time in its 23-year history.

1991 - The emir of Kuwait, Sheikh Jaber al-Ahmed al-Sabah, returned to his war-devastated homeland two weeks to the day after the Gulf War ended.

1991 – "The Birmingham Six," six men (Hugh Callaghan, Patrick Joseph Hill, Gerard Hunter, Richard McIlkenny, William Power, and John Walker) who had been wrongly accused of the 1974 bombing of pubs in Birmingham, England, were freed after 16 years in jail.

NASA Astronaut Norman E. Thagard. Public domain.

1995 – Norman Thagard, the first American astronaut to fly in a Russian rocket, blasted off from the icy windswept plains of Kazakhstan.

1998 - Will Smith's single "Getting' Jiggy Wit It" soared to #1 on *Billboard's* "Hot 100 Chart," and stayed in the top position for 3 weeks.

MARCH 15th

BIRTHDAYS FOR MARCH 15th

1767 Andrew Jackson; 7th U.S. President

1915 Joe E. Ross; American actor and comedian

1916 Harry James; trumpeter, bandleader

1927 Carl Smith; country singer, actor

1932 Alan Bean; astronaut

1933 Ruth Bader Ginsburg; Associate Justice, US Supreme Court Justice

1935 Judd Hirsch; Emmy Award-winning actor

1935 Jimmy Swaggert; evangelist

1936 Don Sundquist; Governor of Tennessee

1940 Phil Lesh; musician, bassist

1941 Mike Love; singer, songwriter

1944 Sly Stone; musician, singer

1947 Ry Cooder; musician, composer

1954 Bob Budiansky; American comic book writer, illustrator, and editor

1955 Dee Snider; composer, singer

1961 Fabio (Lanzoni); model, writer

1961 Terry Cummings; basketball

1962 Terence Trent D'Arby; singer, songwriter

1963 Bret Michaels; American musician

1968 Mark McGrath; singer

EVENTS FOR MARCH 15th

44 BC – Marcus Junius Brutus, Gaius Cassius Longinus, Decimus Junius Brutus and several other Roman senators stabbed Julius Caesar, Dictator of the Roman Republic, to death on the Ides of March.

Depiction of the assassination of Julius Caesar by Michele Cammarano, circa 1798. Public domain.

1493 – Christopher Columbus returned to Spain after his first trip to the Americas.

1783 – In an emotional speech in Newburgh, New York, George Washington asked his officers not to support the Newburgh Conspiracy. Members of the Continental Army had not been paid for a long time, and a group of officers had planned to overthrow Washington's office. The plea was successful and the threatened coup d'état never occurred.

1820 - Maine became the 23rd state of the Union.

1877 - The first cricket match between Australia and England was played in Melbourne, the home side winning by 45 runs.

1892 - The first escalator, the "Reno Inclined Elevator," was patented by Jesse W. Reno of New York.

1906 - Rolls-Royce Ltd. was officially registered with Charles S. Rolls and F. Henry Royce as directors.

1913 - Eleven days after taking office, United States President Woodrow Wilson held the first presidential news conference in which reporters were allowed to ask questions.

1916 - United States President Woodrow Wilson sent 12,000 troops over the border to Mexico in a failed mission to pursue the bandit Pancho Villa.

Woodrow Wilson, the 28th President of the United States' official portrait. Public domain.

1922 - The sultan of Egypt assumed the title of king as Fuad I.

1931 – SS *Viking*, a wooden-hulled whaling ship, exploded off Newfoundland, and killed 27 of the 147 on board.

1937 - The first blood bank was established; it was in the Cook County Hospital in Chicago.

1939 – German troops occupied the remaining part of Bohemia and Moravia; Czechoslovakia ceased to exist.

1948 - Sir Laurence Olivier graced the cover of *LIFE* magazine for starring in Shakespeare's Hamlet.

1952 – In Cilaos, Réunion (an island in the Indian Ocean) 73 inches of rain fell in one day, setting a new world record.

1954 - CBS television debuted its *Morning Show* with host Walter Cronkite.

1956 - The musical *My Fair Lady* opened on Broadway for a 6 ½ year run for 2,717 audiences.

Syngman Rhee in his official portrait from 1956. Public domain.

1956 - The sci-fi film classic, *Forbidden Planet*, starring Walter Pidgeon, Anne Francis, Leslie Nielsen, and Jack Kelly, opened in U.S. theaters.

1960 – Syngman Rhee was elected president of South Korea for a fourth consecutive term.

1964 - Film stars Elizabeth Taylor and Richard Burton were married for the first time in Montreal. They divorced after ten years and then remarried a year later; the second time around, their marriage lasted about ten months. Richard was Elizabeth's 5th and 6th husband.

1968 - Bob Beamon set an indoor long jump record for jumping 27 feet, 2 ¾ inches. His jump was almost as long as a three-story building is tall.

1969 - The hit single "Dizzy," recorded by Tommy Roe, hit *Billboard's* #1 position.

1970 - Boston Bruin Bobby Orr became the first defenseman in NHL history to score 100 points in a season, after scoring four goals in one game against the Detroit Red Wings.

1972 - Directed by Francis Coppola, the Italian family crime epic *The Godfather* opened in United States theaters.

1977 - The first episode of *Eight is Enough* aired on ABC-TV.

1985 – The first Internet domain name was registered (symbolics.com). Although the domain name was in use at the time of this writing, the original company (a computer manufacturer) is now defunct.

President George H. W. Bush and President Gorbachev signing an arms treaty in 1990. Public domain.

1990 – Mikhail Gorbachev was elected the first

executive president of the Soviet Union.

1996 – Pioneering aviation firm Fokker declared bankruptcy ending 77 years of Dutch aircraft manufacturing.

Anthony Fokker sitting in the *Spider*, his first aircraft. Circa 1911. Public domain.

1996 - German authorities issued a warrant for the arrest of Iranian intelligence minister Ali Fallahiyan.

MARCH 16th

BIRTHDAYS FOR MARCH 16th

1739 George Clymer; Signer of the US Declaration of Independence

1751 James Madison; 4th U.S. President

1906 Henny Youngman; comedian, "King of the One Liners"

1911 Josef Mengele; German physician and SS officer

1912 Pat Nixon (Ryan); U.S. First Lady

1926 Jerry Lewis (Jerome Levitch); actor, comedian

1927 Daniel Patrick Moynihan; U.S. Senator from New York

1932 R. Walter Cunningham; astronaut

1941 Chuck Woolery; game show host

1942 Jerry Jeff Walker; singer, guitarist

1949 Erik Estrada; actor

1954 Nancy Wilson; musician, guitarist, singer

1955 Isabelle Huppert; actress

1959 Flavor Flav (William Jonathan Drayton, Jr.); American rapper, and reality TV star

1976 Nick Spano; American actor

EVENTS FOR MARCH 16th

37 AD – Caligula became Roman Emperor after the death of his great uncle, Tiberius.

THE

SCARLET LETTER,

A ROMANCE.

BY

NATHANIEL HAWTHORNE.

BOSTON:
TICKNOR, REED, AND FIELDS.
M DCCC L.

The title page from the first printing of The Scarlett Letter. Public domain.

1802 - The United States Congress passed an act establishing a military academy at West Point, New York.

1850 – Nathaniel Hawthorne's novel *The Scarlet Letter* was published for the first time.

1851 - Spain signed a concordat with the Papacy under which Roman Catholicism became the only authorized faith.

1861 – Edward Clark became the Governor of Texas, replacing Sam Houston, who was evicted from the office for refusing to take an oath of loyalty to the Confederacy.

1871 - The State of Delaware enacted the first fertilizer law. *(Author's note: You may insert your own political joke here.)*

1882 - The United States Senate approved a treaty that allowed the country to join the Red Cross.

1883 - Susan Hayhurst graduated from the Philadelphia College of Pharmacy, and became the first female pharmacy graduate.

1912 – Lawrence Oates, an ill member of Scott's South Pole expedition left the tent during a blizzard saying, "I am just going outside and may be some time." He was never seen alive again.

1926 – The first liquid-fuel rocket was successfully launched by Prof. Robert Goddard at Auburn, Massachusetts.

1935 - German leader Adolf Hitler renounced the disarmament clauses in the Versailles Treaty.

1939 - Slovakia was placed under German control; Hungary annexed Ruthenia (formerly part of Czechoslovakia).

Dr. Robert H. Goddard and a liquid-gasoline rocket in the frame from which it was fired. This photo was taken on the day of the famous launch. Photo from the United States Library of Congress's Prints and Photographs division. Public domain.

1957 - *The Gumby Show*, created by Art Clokey, made its television debut.

1958 – The Ford Motor Company produced its 50-millionth automobile, the Thunderbird, averaging almost a million cars a year since the company's founding.

1964 - The Beatles released their hit single "Can't Buy Me Love." On the reverse side was "You Can't Do That."

1968 – General Motors produced its 100-millionth automobile, the Oldsmobile Toronado.

1971 - The Jackson 5 released "Never Can Say Goodbye."

1976 – Citing personal reasons, British Prime Minister Harold Wilson announced his intention to retire. He was succeeded by James Callaghan on April 5th.

1978 – About 11 years before the Exxon *Valdez*, the supertanker Amoco *Cadiz* split in two after it ran aground on the Portsall Rocks, three miles off the coast of

The broken hull of the Amoco Cadiz, slit in half as it faced the coast of Brittany, France. Public domain.

Brittany, France. Over one million barrels of oil spilled into the sea making it, at the time, the 5th-largest oil spill in history.

1979 - *The China Syndrome* opened in United States movie theaters.

1982 - Soviet President Leonid Brezhnev announced that the Soviet Union was freezing deployment of SS-20 missiles west of the Urals.

1983 - Radio and television personality Arthur Godfrey died at age 79.

1983 – The radio tower "Ismaning," the last wooden radio tower in Germany, was blown up.

1984 - South Africa and Mozambique signed a non-aggression pact near the border town of Komatipoort.

1984 – William Buckley, the CIA station chief in Beirut, Lebanon (not to be confused with the author), was kidnapped by Islamic fundamentalists and died in captivity.

1985 - United States journalist Terry Anderson was kidnapped in Beirut; he was not released until December 4, 1991 after 2,454 days in captivity.

1988 – Lieutenant Colonel Oliver North and Vice Admiral John Poindexter are indicted on charges of conspiracy to defraud the United States.

Oliver North during a 2007 visit to Iraq. Public domain.

1988 – The Kurdish town of Halabjah in Iraq was attacked with a mix of poison gas and nerve agents. Over 5,000 people were killed and 10-thousand more were injured.

1995 – After having rejected it on December 5, 1865, Mississippi formally ratified the 13th Amendment, becoming the last state to approve the abolition of slavery. The 13th Amendment was officially ratified 130 years earlier.

1998 – Pope John Paul II asked God for forgiveness for the inactivity and silence of some Roman Catholics during the Holocaust.

2005 - After a three-month-long criminal trial in Los Angeles Superior Court, a jury acquitted Robert Blake, star of the 1970's television detective show *Baretta*, of the murder of his 44-year-old wife, Bonny Lee Bakley.

2005 – Israel officially handed over Jericho to Palestinian control.

2009 – The Fifth-generation Chevrolet Camaro entered production at the General Motors Oshawa Car Assembly plant in Oshawa, Ontario, Canada.

The 2010 Camaro SS. Photo taken by Nick Ares. Creative Commons License; used by permission.

MARCH 17th

BIRTHDAYS FOR MARCH 17th

1777 Roger Taney; Chief Justice of the U.S. Supreme Court

1834 Gottlieb Daimler; German engineer and inventor

1902 Bobby Jones; golf, PGA Hall of Famer

1907 John Pastore; politician, governor of Rhode Island, U.S. Senator

1919 Nat King Cole (Nathaniel Adams Coles); jazz pianist, bandleader, songwriter

1936 Ken Mattingly; American astronaut

1938 Rudolf Nureyev; Russian ballet dancer

1941 Paul Kantner; American musician

1944 Cito Gaston; baseball

1944 John Sebastian; musician, songwriter

1946 Harold Brown; musician, drummer

1949 Patrick Duffy; actor

1951 Kurt Russell; actor

1952 Susie Allanson; singer

1952 Stan Weir; hockey

1954 Lesley-Anne Down; actress

1955 Gary Sinise; actor

1956 Patrick McDonnell; American cartoonist

1959 Mike Lindup; musician, keyboardist, singer

1959 Danny Ainge; basketball coach, basketball and baseball player

1964 Rob Lowe; actor

1966 Vicki Lewis; actress

1966 Jeremy Sheffield; English actor

1967 Billy Corgan; American musician

EVENTS FOR MARCH 17th

45 BC - Julius Caesar defeated the Pompeians at the battle of Munda in Spain.

1756 – Saint Patrick's Day was celebrated in New York City for the first time (at the Crown and Thistle Tavern).

1762 - The first parade honoring the Catholic feast day of St. Patrick was held in New York City.

1776 - Having seized Dorchester Heights, George Washington forced the British (under William Howe) to evacuate Boston.

1845 - The rubber band was patented in England by Stephen Perry.

1861 - A new united kingdom of Italy was proclaimed by parliament with Victor Emmanuel II as king.

British-born New Zealand boxer Bob Fitzsimmons. Photo courtesy of United States Library of Congress.

1897 - Bob Fitzsimmons knocked out "Gentleman" Jim Corbett to win the world heavyweight title.

1901 – Eleven years after his death, an exhibition of seventy-one Vincent van Gogh paintings in Paris created a sensation.

1906 - In a speech given to the Gridiron Club in Washington, DC, President Theodore Roosevelt coined the word "muckraker."

1910 - Luther and Charlotte Gulick founded the Camp Fire Girls. (The organization was formally announced in 1912.)

1917 – Delta Phi Epsilon was founded at New York University Law School.

1939 - British Prime Minister Neville Chamberlain accused Adolf Hitler of breaking his word, after German troops crossed the Czech frontier.

1941 – The National Gallery of Art was officially opened by United States President Franklin D. Roosevelt.

The west building of the U.S. National Gallery of Art, Washington, DC. Public domain.

1942 – The first Jews from the Lvov Ghetto were gassed at the Belzec death camp in what is today eastern Poland.

1945 – The Ludendorff Bridge in Remagen, Germany collapsed, ten days after its capture. Twenty-eight U.S. Army engineers were killed while working to strengthen the bridge, and 93 others were injured.

1950 – Researchers at the University of California, Berkeley announced the creation of element 98, which they named "Californium."

1958 - The fourth United States satellite to orbit the Earth, Vanguard I, was launched from Cape Canaveral. Although communication with it was lost in 1964, it remains the oldest manmade satellite still in orbit.

1960 – U.S. President Dwight D. Eisenhower signed the National Security Council directive on the anti-Cuban covert action program. That signing ultimately lead to the Bay of Pigs Invasion.

1963 - On Bali, the volcano Mount Agung erupted, and killed no less than 1,500 people.

1966 – The submarine DSV *Alvin* found a missing American hydrogen bomb off the coast of Spain in the Mediterranean.

This is a panorama of the *Alvin* on the stern of the R/V *Atlantis* following a dive. Photo by Kirt L. Onthank. Creative Commons License; used by permission.

1967 - *Peanuts* comic strip characters, Snoopy and Charlie Brown, were on the cover of *LIFE* magazine.

1968 - Violent demonstrations against the Vietnam War erupted outside the American embassy in London. All in all, more than 10-thousand people participated in the protest.

Golda Meier in her school portrait taken in 1914 while she was attending college in Wisconsin. Public domain.

1969 – Golda Meir was sworn in as Israel's fourth premier.

1970 - Eddie Holman was awarded a gold record for the single, "Hey There Lonely Girl."

1978 - *American Hot Wax* opened in United States theaters.

1985 – Serial killer Richard Ramirez, aka the "Night Stalker," committed the first two murders in his Los Angeles, California murder spree.

1995 - President Haydar Aliyev of Azerbaijan survived a coup attempt when troops crushed a revolt by an elite police unit.

2000 – More than 800 members of the Ugandan cult Movement for the "Restoration of the Ten Commandments of God" died in what is considered to be a mass murder and suicide orchestrated by leaders of the cult.

2003 – British Cabinet Minister Robin Cook resigned over government plans for the war with Iraq.

2004 – Unrest in Kosovo resulted in more than 22 killed, 200 wounded, and the destruction of 35 Serb Orthodox shrines in Kosovo and two mosques in Belgrade and Nis.

2008 – New York State Governor Eliot Spitzer resigned after a scandal involving a high-end prostitute. David Paterson became New York State governor.

MARCH 18th

BIRTHDAYS FOR MARCH 18th

1496 Mary Tudor; daughter of Henry VII of England and queen consort of Louis XII of France

1782 John Calhoun; 7th U.S. Vice President

1837 Grover Cleveland; 22nd and 24th U.S. President

1844 Nikolai Rimski-Korsakov; composer

1858 Rudolf Diesel; German inventor, inventor of the diesel engine

1877 Edgar Cayce; American psychic

1909 Ernest Gallo; American winemaker

1911 Smiley Burnette (Lester Alvin Burnett); actor

1923 Andy Granatelli; auto racer

1926 Peter Graves (Aurness); actor

1927 George Plimpton; author

1927 George Kander; composer

1932 John Updike; writer

1936 Frederik Willem de Klerk; South African President

1937 Mark Donohue; auto racer, Indianapolis 500 winner

1938 Charley Pride; country singer, semipro baseball

1941 Margie Bowes; country entertainer

1941 Wilson Pickett; singer, Rock and Roll Hall of Famer

1945 Michael Reagan; American radio host and adopted son of Ronald Reagan

1951 Ben Cohen; American co-founder of Ben & Jerry's ice cream

1956 Ingemar Stenmark; skier

1962 Irene Cara; singer, actress

1963 Vanessa Williams; singer, actress, ex-Miss America

1964 Bonnie Blair; Olympic Gold medalist speed skater

1970 Queen Latifah; rap artist, actress

1972 Dane Cook; American comedian and actor

EVENTS FOR MARCH 18th

1229 - Roman Emperor Frederick II crowned himself king of Jerusalem during the Sixth Crusade.

1314 – Jacques de Molay, the 23rd and the last Grand Master of the Knights Templar, was burned at the stake after recanting a confession that was earlier coerced through torture.

1766 - Britain repealed the Stamp Act, despised in its colonies, but retained the right to impose taxes in the future.

Portrait of Jacques de Molay from Bibliotheque Nationale de France. Public domain.

1813 - David Melville, from Newport, Rhode Island, patented the gas streetlight.

1834 - In Dorset, England six laborers were sentenced to seven years banishment to a penal colony in Australia for forming a trade union.

1850 – American Express was founded by Henry Wells and William Fargo. Before offering varying financial services, the company began as an express delivery service. Two years to the date later, the same two men founded . . . (See next entry.)

1852 - Businessmen in New York established Wells, Fargo and Company, destined to become the leading freight and banking company of the West.

A shipping receipt dated August 6, 1853. Public domain.

1871 – By declaration of the Paris Commune, President of the French Republic, Adolphe Thiers, ordered the evacuation of Paris.

1893 – Former Governor General Lord Stanley pledged to donate a silver challenge cup, later named after him, as an award for the best hockey team in

Canada; originally presented to amateur champions, the Stanley Cup has been awarded to the top pro team since 1910, and since 1926, only to National Hockey League teams.

1902 - Operatic tenor Enrico Caruso, one of the first musicians to document his voice on the gramophone, made his first phonograph recording.

1906 – Powered by a carbonic acid gas engine, Traian Vuia flew a heavier-than-air aircraft for 65 feet at an altitude of almost 4 feet.

Traian Vula's flying machine. Public domain.

1911 - Irving Berlin received a copyright for the song "Alexander's Ragtime Band," which some consider to be the biggest pop song of the early 20th century.

1913 - King George I of Greece was assassinated at Salonika.

1922 - Mahatma Gandhi was sentenced to six years in prison for his civil disobedience campaign.

1925 – The Tri-State Tornado hit the midwestern states of Missouri, Illinois, and Indiana. Almost 700 people were confirmed dead, but some news reports cited a death rate of over a thousand.

FIRST PICTURES OF STORM DISASTER
HERALD⚡EXAMINER

1,000 DEAD, 3,000 HURT LATEST TOLL OF TORNADO

In the Twinkling of an Eye, Murphysboro Was No More

Front page from the *Herald Examiner*. Copyright 1925 by the *Herald Examiner*, used by permission.

1931 - The razor company Schick, Inc., displayed the first electric shaver.

1937 – A natural gas leak caused an explosion, destroying the London School of New London, Texas. Almost 300 people were killed including students, teachers, and parents who were in an adjacent building waiting for a meeting to begin.

1937 – Powered only by a pilot pumping bicycle-type pedals; the *Pedaliante* flew for almost a mile.

The *Pedaliante*, designed and built by Italian-American aerospace engineer and aviation pioneer Enea Bossi Sr, 1937. Public domain.

1940 - Hitler and Mussolini met at the Brenner Pass in the Alps and agreed that Italy would eventually join the war.

1944 – The eruption of Mount Vesuvius in Italy killed 26 and caused thousands to flee their homes.

1944 - For the first time since World War II started, alarm clocks went back on sale in the United States.

1962 - The war in Algeria ended when agreements were signed with the French leading to Algeria's independence.

1965 – Soviet cosmonaut Aleksei Leonov made the first spacewalk.

1967 - The oil tanker *Torrey Canyon* was wrecked off the Cornish coast of England and spilled 919,000 barrels of oil into the sea.

1970 - Brook Benton was awarded a gold record for the single, "Rainy Night in Georgia."

1978 - The Bee Gees began an eight-week stay in the #1 position on *Billboard's* Hot 100 music chart with "Night Fever."

Aleksei Leonov exits *Voskhod 2* for a spacewalk. Public domain.

1985 - ABC announced its plans to merge with Capital Cities Communications to form Cap Cities/ABC. To buy into the merger, Capital Cities paid a reported $3.5 billion.

1989 – In Egypt, a 4,400-year-old mummy was found nearby the Pyramid of Cheops.

1990 – Shortly after midnight on the morning of March 18, 1990, thieves disguised as police officers talked their way into the Isabella Stewart Gardner Museum in Boston, Massachusetts. They handcuffed the two on-duty security guards out of sight and then stole thirteen works of art valued at over $500 million.

1997 – The tail of a Russian Antonov An-24 charter plane broke off while en-route to Turkey causing the plane to crash, killing all 50 on board. This led to the grounding of all An-24s.

2002 – "Operation Anaconda" ended (it began on March 2) after killing 500 Taliban and al Qaeda fighters with 11 allied troop fatalities.

2003 – FBI agents raided the corporate headquarters of HealthSouth Corporation in Birmingham, Alabama on suspicion of massive corporate fraud led by the company's top executives.

2002 – Thirteen year-old Brittanie Cecil died, two days after being struck in the head by a puck at a Columbus Blue Jackets ice hockey game. Brittanie's death forced the National Hockey League to take new precautions regarding fan safety.

2003 – British Sign Language was recognized as an official British language.

2005 – Terri Schiavo's feeding tube was removed at the request of her husband. Terri lived until the end of the month.

MARCH 19th

BIRTHDAYS FOR MARCH 19th

1590 William Bradford; governor, sailed on the Mayflower

1734 Thomas McKean; governor, Signer of the US Declaration of Independence

1813 David Livingstone; missionary, explorer

1848 Wyatt Earp; frontiersman, lawman, gunfighter

1860 William Jennings Bryan; politician, member of U.S. Congress

1864 Charles M. Russell; artist

1891 Earl Warren; Chief Justice of the U.S. Supreme Court

1892 James Van Fleet; 4-star U.S. Army General

1904 John Sirica; judge, Watergate trials

1928 Patrick McGoohan; actor, director

1933 Phyllis Newman; actress

1933 Renee Taylor; Emmy Award-winning writer, actress

1936 Ursula Andress; actress

1944 Lynda Bird Johnson; daughter of U.S. President Lyndon B. Johnson

1946 Paul Atkinson; musician, guitarist

1946 Ruth Pointer; singer

1947 Glenn Close; Tony Award-winning actress

1951 Derek Longmuir; musician, drummer (Bay City Rollers)

1952 Chris Brubeck; composer, musician, trombonist

1955 Bruce Willis; Emmy Award-winning actor

1959 Terry Hall; singer

EVENTS FOR MARCH 19th

1831 - The first bank robbery in the United States was reported at the City Bank of New York City. The first bank robber was Edward Smith who made off with $245,000.

1842 - French writer Honore de Balzac's play *Les Ressources de Quinola* opened to an empty house thanks to a failed publicity stunt. Hoping to create a buzz for the play, the writer circulated a rumor that tickets were sold out. Most of his fans believed the claim and stayed home.

1861 - The Maori insurrection in New Zealand ended.

1863 – The SS *Georgiana*, said to have been the most powerful Confederate cruiser, was destroyed on her maiden voyage with a cargo of munitions, medicines and merchandise then valued at over $1,000,000.

1915 – Pluto was photographed for the first time but was not yet recognized as a planet.

1916 – Eight American planes take off in pursuit of Pancho Villa, the first United States air-combat mission in history.

1918 – The U.S. Congress established time zones and approved daylight saving time.

1920 - The United States refused to sign the Versailles Treaty and joined the League of Nations for the second time. The U.S. had rejected the treaty in November of the previous year.

1931 - The Nevada state legislature voted to legalize gambling.

1932 – Australia's Sydney Harbor Bridge was officially opened.

Arial view of the Sydney Harbor Bridge (please note the Opera House on the left). Copyrighted photo taken by Rodney Haywood. Used by permission.

1941 – The 99th Pursuit Squadron, also known as the Tuskegee Airmen, the first all-black unit of the Army Air Corp, was activated.

1943 – Frank Nitti, the Chicago Outfit Boss after Al Capone, committed suicide at the Chicago Central Rail yard.

1944 - In World War II, under pressure from Hitler, Hungary allowed German troops to cross the border into the country.

1945 – A dive-bomber hit the aircraft carrier USS *Franklin* off the coast of Japan, killing 724 of her crew. Badly damaged, the ship was able to return to the U.S. under her own power.

1949 - The American Museum of Atomic Energy opened in Oak Ridge, Tennessee and was later renamed the American Museum of Science and Energy.

Candid photo of Edgar Rice Burroughs. Date unknown. Public domain.

1950 – Edgar Rice Burroughs, the creator of the jungle hero Tarzan, died.

1951 - Herman Wouk's novel, *The Caine Mutiny*, was published.

1953 - For the very first time, the *Academy Awards* ceremony was aired on national television by NBC.

1954 – Willie Mosconi set a world record by running 526 consecutive balls without a miss during a straight pool exhibition at East High Billiard Club in Springfield, Ohio. The record still stood as of the date of this writing.

1954 - The first televised prizefight shown in color was broadcast from New York's Madison Square Garden. (Joey Giardello v. Willie Tory – Joey won.)

1954 - Lt. Col. John L. Stapp became the fastest human to date when his rocket sled topped out at 632 miles per hour at the Holloman Air Base Development Center; Alamogordo, New Mexico.

1957 – With a $1,000 cash deposit against a sale price of $102,500, Elvis Presley agreed to purchase the home called Graceland.

1958 – A fire at The Monarch Underwear Company in Manhattan left 24 dead and 15 injured.

1964 - The Great St. Bernard Tunnel under the Alps, between Switzerland and Italy, was opened to traffic.

The Emley Moor TV-mast before the ice storm. Photo by Alan Zomerfeld.

1969 – The 1,263 ft. tall TV-mast at Emley Moor, United Kingdom, collapsed due to ice build-up.

1971 - An earthquake set off a series of calamities: a landslide, flood, and an avalanche. The three events resulted in the destruction of the town of Chungar, Peru, and the death of 600 of its inhabitants.

1972 - A Treaty of friendship and mutual defense was signed between India and Bangladesh.

After the ice storm. Photo by Gerald England. Both photos Creative Commons License; used by permission.

1977 - The final episode of *The Mary Tyler Moore Show* aired on CBS.

1978 - United Nations Security Council voted to send an Interim Force to Lebanon after a massive Israeli air raid on March 14th.

1979 – The United States House of Representatives began broadcasting its day-to-day business via the cable television network C-SPAN.

1987 – Televangelist Jim Bakker resigned as head of the PTL Club due to a brewing sex scandal; he handed over control to Jerry Falwell.

2003 – United States President George W. Bush ordered the start of war against Iraq.

2004 – A semi-trailer truck and a bus crashed head-on in Äänekoski, Finland. 24 people were killed and 13 injured.

2004 – A Swedish DC-3 shot down by a Russian MiG-15 in 1952 over the Baltic Sea was finally recovered after years of work. The remains of the three crewmen were left in place, pending further investigations.

2004 – Taiwanese president Chen Shui-bian is shot just before the country's presidential election on March 20.

MARCH 20th

BIRTHDAYS FOR MARCH 20th

1904 B.F. (Burrhus Frederic) Skinner; psychologist

1906 Ozzie Nelson; bandleader, actor

1908 Sir Michael Redgrave; actor

1922 Larry Elgart; American saxophonist and bandleader

1922 Carl Reiner; writer, director

1928 Fred Rogers; TV host

1931 Hal Linden (Harold Lipshitz); actor

1937 Jerry Reed; singer, songwriter

1943 Paul Junger Witt; American TV producer

1948 John de Lancie; American actor

1948 Bobby Orr; Hockey Hall of Famer

1950 William Hurt; actor

1950 Carl Palmer; English drummer (Emerson, Lake & Palmer)

1957 Spike Lee; director

1957 Theresa Russell; actress

1958 Holly Hunter; Academy Award-winning actress

1959 Sting (Steven James Borden Sr.); American professional wrestler

1961 Slim Jim Phantom (Jim McDonell); musician, drummer

1963 Kathy Ireland; American model and actress

EVENTS FOR MARCH 20th

1602 - The Dutch East India Company was established.

Engraving of Sir Walter Raleigh. Picture courtesy of United States' Library of Congress. Public domain.

1616 – Sir Walter Raleigh was freed from the Tower of London after 13 years of imprisonment.

1815 - Napoleon Bonaparte entered Paris and began his "Hundred Days" rule.

1816 - The Supreme Court affirmed its right to review state court decisions.

1852 – Harriet Beecher Stowe's anti-slavery novel *Uncle Tom's Cabin* was first published in book form.

1865 - John Wilkes Booth's plan to abduct President Abraham Lincoln was thwarted when Lincoln failed to appear at the Soldier's Home near Washington, DC.

1914 - The first international figure skating championship was held in New Haven, Connecticut.

1916 – Albert Einstein published his general theory of relativity.

1920 - The first flight between Cape Town, South Africa and Cairo was completed by C.J. Brand. The entire journey took about 72 hours.

1922 – The USS *Langley* (CV-1) is commissioned as the first United States Navy aircraft carrier.

The USS Langley sailing out of San Diego. Public domain.

1923 – The Arts Club of Chicago hosted the opening of Pablo Picasso's first United States showing. They billed the event as "Original Drawings by Pablo Picasso"

1933 – Giuseppe Zangara was executed in Florida's electric chair for fatally shooting Anton Cermak (then Mayor of Chicago) in an assassination attempt against President Franklin D. Roosevelt.

1933 - The first German concentration camp was opened at Dachau.

1942 – General Douglas MacArthur, at Terowie, South Australia, made his famous speech regarding the fall of the Philippines, in which he said: "I came out of Bataan and I shall return."

1948 – With a Musicians Union ban lifted, the first telecasts of classical music in the United States, under Eugene Ormandy and Arturo Toscanini, were given on CBS and NBC.

1952 - Humphrey Bogart won an Academy Award for Best Actor as the result of his performance in *African Queen*.

1953 - The Soviet government announced that Nikita Khrushchev had been selected as one of five men named to the new office of Secretariat of the Communist Party.

1964 – The precursor of the European Space Agency, ESRO (European Space Research Organization), was established via an agreement signed on June 14, 1962.

1967 – Twiggy, the first prominent teenage model, arrived in the United States.

1969 – Yoko Ono became John Lennon's second wife.

1971 - Janis Joplin's recording, "Me and Bobby McGee," went to #1.

1974 – Ian Ball attempted, but failed, to kidnap Her Royal Highness Princess Anne and her husband Captain Mark Phillips in The Mall, outside Buckingham Palace, London.

1976 - Newspaper heiress Patricia Hearst was convicted of armed robbery for her part in a San Francisco bank holdup. She was sentenced to 35 years imprisonment, but her sentence was later commuted to seven years.

1985 – Libby Riddles became the first woman to win the 1,135-mile Iditarod Trail Sled Dog Race. She completed the course in 18 days, 20 minutes, and 17 seconds.

1987 - The Food and Drug Administration approved the sale of AZT, a drug shown to prolong the lives of some AIDS patients.

1990 – Ferdinand Marcos's widow, Imelda Marcos, went on trial for bribery, embezzlement, and racketeering. All of her cases were subsequently dismissed in 2008.

1995 – In Tokyo, 12 people were killed, and more than 1,300 others were sickened when packages containing the poisonous gas sarin leaked on five separate subway trains.

The wanted poster that was widely circulated in Japan for the suspects in the Tokyo gas attack. Creative Commons License; used by permission.

1997 – The Liggett Group, the makers of Chesterfield, L&M, and Eve cigarettes, settled 22 state lawsuits by agreeing to warn on every pack that smoking is addictive and admitting the industry markets cigarettes to teen-agers. Plaintiffs in the lawsuit were also paid 25 percent of Liggett's pre-tax earnings for twenty-five years.

1999 – Legoland California, the only Legoland outside of Europe, opened in Carlsbad, California.

2000 – Jamil Abdullah Al-Amin, a former Black Panther once known as H. Rap Brown (at birth he was named Hubert Gerold Brown), was captured after murdering Georgia sheriff's deputy Ricky Kinchen and critically wounding Deputy Aldranon English.

2003 – In the early hours of the morning, the United States and three other countries begin military operations in Iraq.

2004 – Stephen Harper won the leadership of the newly created Conservative Party of Canada, becoming the party's first leader.

2005 – A magnitude 6.6 earthquake hit Fukuoka, Japan, its first major quake in over 100 years. One person was killed; hundreds were injured and evacuated.

2006 – Cyclone Larry made landfall in eastern Australia, destroying most of the country's banana crop.

2006 – Over 150 Chadian soldiers were killed in eastern Chad by members of the rebel UFDC. The rebel movement sought to overthrow Chadian president Idriss Deby.

MARCH 21st

BIRTHDAYS FOR MARCH 21st

1685 Johann Sebastian Bach; composer

1713 Francis Lewis; Signer of the US Declaration of Independence

1806 Benito Juarez; former President of Mexico

1869 Florenz Ziegfeld; producer

1910 Julio Gallo; vintner, Ernest & Julio Gallo Winery

1918 Sir Charles Thompson; musician, pianist, organist, composer

1930 James Coco; actor

1944 Manny Sanguillen; baseball

1945 Rose Stone; musician, pianist

1946 Timothy Dalton; actor

1946 Timothy Dalton; British actor

1947 Bill Plummer; baseball

1949 Eddie Money; American musician

1950 Roger Hodgson; musician, guitarist

1951 John Hicks; football

1951 Russell Thompkins, Jr.; singer

1958 Gary Oldman; actor

1959 Jay Hilgenberg; football

1962 Matthew Broderick; actor

1962 Rosie O'Donnell; actress, TV host

1966 Cynthia Geary; actress

1978 Kevin Federline; American dancer/hip hop artist

EVENTS FOR MARCH 21st

1413 – Henry V became the King of England.

1556 - The Archbishop of Canterbury, Thomas Cranmer, was burned at the stake as a heretic.

1804 - The French civil code, the Code Napoleon, was adopted as French civil law.

1844 – The Bahá'í calendar began. This is the first day of the first year of the Bahá'í calendar. It is annually celebrated by members of the Bahá'í Faith as the Bahá'í New Year or Náw-Rúz.

Portrait of William Miller. Public domain.

1844 – The original date predicted by William Miller for the return of Christ. He also predicted the date would be in October in the same year. His predictions were not correct. (William Miller was an American Baptist preacher, whose followers have been termed Millerites. He is credited with the beginning of the Adventism movement of the 1830s and 1840s in North America.)

1859 – The Philadelphia Zoo, America's 1st zoo, was chartered by the Commonwealth of Pennsylvania as the Zoological Society of Philadelphia.

1871 - Chancellor Otto von Bismarck opened the first Reichstag (parliament) in the newly created German Reich.

1871 – Journalist Henry Morton Stanley began his trek to find the missionary and explorer David Livingstone. Stanley is often remembered for the words uttered to Livingstone upon finding him, "Dr. Livingstone, I presume?"

1905 - Pennsylvania passed sterilization legislation in a bill called "An Act for the Prevention of Idiocy." This bill would call for forced vasectomies of mental patients. The Governor vetoed the bill later that same month.

1913 – Over 360 people were killed and 20,000 homes were destroyed in the Great Dayton Flood in Dayton, Ohio.

**Flooding through the downtown area of Dayton. During the Great Dayton Flood.
Public domain.**

1918 – During World War I the first phase of the German Spring Offensive, "Operation Michael," began.

1919 – The Hungarian Soviet Republic was established and became the first Communist government to be formed in Europe after the October Revolution in Russia.

1925 - Lowell Thomas was first heard on KDKA radio in Pittsburgh, Pennsylvania; his topic was "Man's First Flight Around the World."

1928 – Charles Lindbergh was presented the Medal of Honor for the first solo trans-Atlantic flight.

1933 – Construction of Dachau, the first Nazi Germany concentration camp, was completed and the camp opened the next day.

1935 – Shah Reza Pahlavi formally asked the international community to call Persia by its native name, Iran, which means "Land of the Aryans."

Carlos Torres Morales, a photo journalist for the newspaper *El Imparcial* took this photograph when the shooting began. Public domain.

1937 – Eighteen people and a 7-year old girl in Ponce, Puerto Rico, are gunned down by a police squad acting under orders of US-appointed PR Governor, Blanton C. Winship during an event known as "the Ponce Massacre."

1945 - British warplanes destroyed Gestapo headquarters in Copenhagen during Operation Carthage. During the attack, the planes also struck a nearby school and killed over a hundred civilians.

1952 - Kwame Nkrumah became prime minister of the Gold Coast (later known as Ghana), the first African to be elected prime minister south of the Sahara.

1952 – Alan Freed presented "The Moondog Coronation Ball," generally accepted as the first major rock and roll concert, in Cleveland, Ohio.

1953 - As part of the Anglo-Egyptian plan for the future of Sudan, a self-government statute was signed leading to elections and independence.

1956 - One of the nominees for the *Academy Award* ceremony held on this date was the late James Dean, the first actor to be nominated posthumously. He had been nominated for his role in the movie *East of Eden*. (In his category, Mr. Dean lost to Ernest Borgnine for his role in *Marty*.)

1961 - The Beatles debuted at Liverpool's Cavern Club, where they would become regulars in a few months. Their first engagement was a lunchtime session and they made their evening debut one month later.

1963 – Alcatraz Prison in San Francisco Bay closed when the last 27 prisoners were transferred.

Panoramic photo of Alcatraz, copyright 2006 by Carlos Torres Morales. Creative Commons License: used by permission.

1965 – NASA launched Ranger 9 which was the last in a series of unmanned lunar space probes.

1965 - Martin Luther King led 3,200 people in the start of a civil rights march from Selma to Montgomery, Alabama.

1968 - Israel launched an attack on Karameh in the Jordan Valley in retaliation for raids and sabotage in the occupied territories.

1970 - The Beatles set a new record as "Let It Be" entered the *Billboard* chart at #6, making it to date the highest debuting position ever for a record.

1970 – The first Earth Day proclamation was issued by San Francisco Mayor Joseph Alioto.

The Southfork ranch near Plano, TX where *Dallas* was filmed. As of this writing, this building was being used as an event center. Public domain.

1980 – On the season finale of the soap opera *Dallas*, the infamous character J.R. Ewing was shot by an unseen assailant, leading to the catch phrase "Who Shot JR?" The name of the episode was "A House Divided."

1980 – US President Jimmy Carter announced a United States boycott of the 1980 Summer Olympics in Moscow to protest the Soviet Invasion of Afghanistan.

1985 – Canadian paraplegic athlete and humanitarian Rick Hansen began his circumnavigation of the globe in a wheelchair in the name of spinal cord injury medical research. His journey took two years to complete and was called "The Man in Motion Tour."

1989 – *Sports Illustrated* reported allegations that connected baseball player Pete Rose to baseball gambling.

1989 - Australian Prime Minister Bob Hawke wept on television as he admitted to an extra-marital affair.

1990 – Namibia became independent after 75 years of South African rule.

1997 - Jennifer Lopez and Edward James Olmos starred in the newly released film *Selena*.

1997 – In a Tel Aviv, Israel coffee shop a suicide bomber killed 3 and injured 49.

1999 – Bertrand Piccard and Brian Jones became the first to circumnavigate the Earth in a hot air balloon.

Piccard and Jones each submitted the same manuscript to two different publishers under two different titles. Both were published. Public domain.

2002 – In Pakistan, Ahmed Omar Saeed Sheikh, along with three other suspects, was charged with murder for taking part in the kidnapping and killing of *Wall Street Journal* reporter Daniel Pearl.

2002 – British schoolgirl Amanda Dowler was abducted in broad daylight on her way home from Heathside School in Walton-on-Thames, Surrey. Amanda's body was found in a nearby wooded area six months later.

2006 – Immigrant workers, constructing the Burj Khalifa and a new terminal of Dubai International Airport, rioted and caused $1 million in damage. The reported reason for the riot: the workers were upset over buses that were delayed for the end of their shifts.

MARCH 22nd

BIRTHDAYS FOR MARCH 22nd

1887 Chico Marx; comedian

1908 Louis L'Amour; American author

1912 Karl Malden (Mladen Sekulovich); actor

1920 Werner Klemperer; Emmy Award-winning actor

1923 Marcel Marceau; mime

1924 Bill Wendell (William Joseph Wenzel, Jr.); announcer

1924 Allen Newharth; USA Today founder

1930 Pat Robertson; TV evangelist

1930 Stephen Sondheim; composer

1931 William Shatner; actor

1933 May Britt; actress

1934 Orrin Hatch; U.S. Senator

1935 Gene Oliver; baseball

1941 Jeremy Clyde; British actor and musician (Chad and Jeremy)

1943 George Benson; singer, guitarist

1946 Don Chaney; basketball

1946 Harry Vanda; musician, guitarist

1948 Wolf Blitzer; American television journalist

1948 Randy Hobbs; musician, bassist

1948 Andrew Lloyd Webber; composer

1952 Bob Costas; sportscaster

1955 Lena Olin; actress

1957 Stephanie Mills; actress

1959 Matthew Modine; actor

1972 Elvis Stojko; skater

1976 Reese Witherspoon; actress

EVENTS FOR MARCH 22nd

1630 – The Massachusetts Bay Colony outlawed the possession of cards, dice, and gaming tables.

1638 – Anne Hutchinson was expelled from Massachusetts Bay Colony for religious dissent. Hutchinson held Bible meetings for women that soon appealed to men as well. Eventually, she went beyond Bible study to proclaim her own theological interpretations of sermons.

1765 – The British Parliament passes the Stamp Act that introduces a tax to be levied directly on its American colonies. Many colonists considered it a violation of their rights as Englishmen to be taxed without their consent.

1848 - After an insurrection, the Venetian Republic declared its independence from Austria.

1859 - The first political party dedicated to the working class, the Political Labour League of Victoria, was founded in Melbourne.

1871 – In North Carolina, William Woods Holden became the first governor of a U.S. state to be removed from office by impeachment.

1873 – A law was approved by the Spanish National Assembly in Puerto Rico to abolish slavery.

1894 – The first playoff game for the Stanley Cup began; Montreal defeated Ottowa, 3-1.

1895 – Auguste and Louis Lumiere gave the first demonstration of motion pictures using celluloid film in Paris.   Their demonstration consisted of ten movies each one running only about a minute.

The first known movie poster used to promote a showing of the Lumiere Brothers' motion pictures. Public domain.

1919 - The first international airline service was instituted between Paris and Brussels on a weekly schedule.

1941 – The Grand Coulee Dam in Washington, United States, began generating electricity.

1943 – The entire population of Khatyn in Belarus was burnt alive by German occupation forces during World War II. The 118th Schutzmannschaft battalion, a unit mostly composed of criminals recruited for anti-partisan duties, entered the village and drove the inhabitants from their houses and into a shed, which was then covered with straw and set on fire. One hundred forty-five people, including 75 children, were killed.

1944 - Germany announced its occupation of Hungary and the formation of a new government under Prime Minister Döme Sztójay.

1945 - The Arab League was formed in Cairo by Egypt, Iraq, Jordan, Lebanon, and Syria.

1948 - *The Voice of Firestone* became the first commercial radio program carried simultaneously on AM and FM radio stations.

1958 - Movie producer Mike Todd (Elizabeth Taylor's 3rd husband) and three other passengers were killed when the aircraft they were in experienced engine failure and crashed.

1958 - South Carolina police pulled over Alabama auto racer J. Wilson Morris for exceeding the speed limit, as Morris attempted to race across the state in record time. The police held the 19-year-old Morris in jail for two days and that scared him so bad that he finished his trip on the bus.

1960 – Arthur Leonard Schawlow and Charles Hard Townes received the first patent for a laser.

1972 - The Equal Rights Amendment was passed by the U.S. Senate and sent to the states for ratification. The amendment fell short of the requisite three-fourths of the states and failed.

1975 – A fire at the Browns Ferry Nuclear Power Plant in Decatur, Alabama caused a dangerous reduction in cooling water levels. The fire began when a worker using a candle to search for air leaks accidentally set a temporary cable seal on fire.

1977 - Comedian Lily Tomlin debuted on Broadway, as *Lily Tomlin on Stage* opened.

1978 - Karl Wallenda, the 73-year-old patriarch of the famous "Flying Wallendas" high-wire act, fell to his death while attempting to walk a cable in Puerto Rico.

1979 - Sir Richard Sykes, Britain's Ambassador to the Netherlands, was shot dead by Irish terrorists in The Hague.

1980 - Pink Floyd began a 4-week run in the #1 spot *Billboard's* Hot 100 Chart with, "Another Brick in the Wall."

1981 - United States Postage rates climbed from 15-cents to 18-cents an ounce.

1982 – NASA's Space Shuttle *Columbia*, was launched from the Kennedy Space Center on its third mission. This was the first time the shuttle had launched with an unpainted fuel tank.

The 1982 launch of the Space Shuttle *Columbia*. Note the dark main fuel tank. Up until now the tank had always been painted white. Public domain.

1983 - The Pentagon awarded a

production contract worth more than $1 billion to AM General Corporation to develop 55,000 High Mobility Multipurpose Wheeled Vehicles (HMMWV). Nicknamed the "Humvee," the vehicle was eventually redesigned into a civilian version called, "The Hummer."

1984 – Teachers at the McMartin preschool in Manhattan Beach, California were charged with satanic ritual abuse of the children in the school. The charges were later dropped as completely unfounded.

1987 - A 3,100-ton pile of rotting garbage left Islip, New York to look for a landfill willing to take its contents. The barge traveled up and down the eastern coast looking for a place to dump its cargo. Finally in October of that year, it landed at Brooklyn where it was incinerated. The resulting ashes were buried where it originated, Islip.

1997 – The Comet Hale-Bopp made its closest approach to earth.

2004 – Ahmed Yassin, co-founder and leader of the Palestinian Sunni Islamist terrorist group Hamas, and bodyguards were killed in the Gaza Strip when they were hit by Israeli Air Force AH-64 Apache fired Hellfire missiles.

2006 – BC Ferries' M/V *Queen of the North* ran aground on Gil Island British Columbia, Canada and sank; 101 on board, 2 presumed deaths.

2006 – Three Christian Peacemaker Teams Hostages were freed by British forces in Baghdad after 118 days captivity and the death of their colleague, American Tom Fox.

2009 – Mount Redoubt, a volcano in Alaska began erupting after a prolonged period of unrest.

MARCH 23rd

BIRTHDAYS FOR MARCH 23rd

1645 William Kidd; Scottish sailor

1823 Schuyler Colfax; 17th U.S. Vice President

1900 Erich Fromm; psychoanalyst

1905 Joan Crawford (Lucille Fay LeSueur); Academy Award-winning actress

1910 Akira Kurosawa; film director

1912 Wernher Von Braun; scientist

1914 Milbourne Christopher; American illusionist

1922 Marty Allen; American comedian and actor

1931 Warren Godfrey; hockey

1949 Ric Ocasek; musician, singer

1951 Ron Jaworski; football

1953 Chaka Khan (Yvette Marie Stevens); singer

1954 Moses Eugene Malone; basketball

1957 Teresa Ganzel; actress

1957 Amanda Plummer; Tony Award-winning actress

1965 Richard Greico; actor

1965 Marti Pellow; singer

1973 Jason Kidd; basketball

1976 Jayson Blair; American journalist and author

1976 Keri Russell; actress

1978 Perez Hilton; American blogger and television persona

1990 Princess Eugenie; British royalty

EVENTS FOR MARCH 23rd

1743 – Handel's *Messiah* debuted in London. A precedent was set as King George II stood during the "Hallelujah Chorus." From that date forward, people still stand when the famous chorus is performed in concert.

1775 - Patrick Henry told the Virginia Convention "Give me liberty, or give me death!"

1801 – Tsar Paul I of Russia was struck with a sword, then strangled, and finally trampled to death in his bedroom at St. Michael's Castle.

1806 – After traveling through the Louisiana Purchase and reaching the Pacific Ocean, explorers Lewis and Clark and their "Corps of Discovery" began their arduous journey home.

**Portrait of Elisha Otis.
Public domain.**

1839 - The initials "O.K." were first published in *The Boston Morning Post*. Meant as an abbreviation for "oll korrect," a popular slang misspelling of "all correct," OK steadily made its way into the everyday speech of Americans.

1857 – Elisha Otis's first elevator was installed at 488 Broadway New York City.

1858 - Eleazer A. Gardner, of Philadelphia, Pennsylvania, was awarded patent #19736 for the cable streetcar that, even as of this writing, runs on overhead cables in some cities.

1861 - John D. Defrees became the first Superintendent of Public Printing in the United States Government Printing Office.

1868 – The University of California was founded in Oakland, California when the Organic Act was signed into law.

1880 – John Stevens, of Neenah, Wisconsin, patented the grain-crushing roll.

1909 – Theodore Roosevelt left New York for a post-presidency safari in Africa. The trip was sponsored by the Smithsonian Institution and National Geographic Society.

1918 – The giant German Howitzer, "Big Bertha," shelled Paris from 75 miles away.

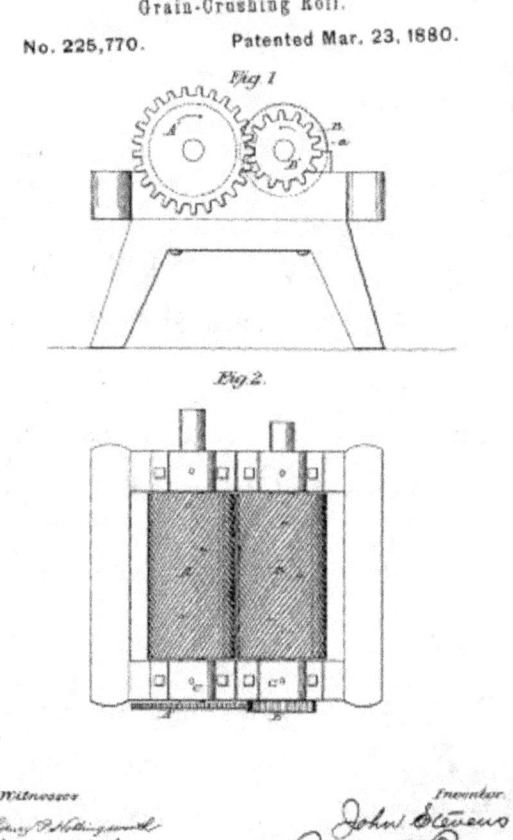

Original patent drawings for the grain crushing roll. Public domain

1919 - Benito Mussolini founded his own party in Italy, the Fasci di Combattimento.

1933 - The German parliament passed the Enabling Bill, giving "Adolf Hitler" and the Nazi party the dictatorial powers they had been seeking.

1940 - *Truth or Consequences*, hosted by Ralph Edwards, was first heard on radio via the NBC Red Network.

1950 - *Beat the Clock*, starring radio's first "Superman," Bud Collyer, debuted on CBS-TV.

1956 - Under its new constitution Pakistan became an Islamic republic, with Maj. Gen. Iskander Mirza as first provisional president.

The NS Savannah preparing to sail underneath the Golden Gate Bridge. Public domain.

1962 – NS *Savannah*, the first nuclear-powered cargo-passenger ship, was launched as a showcase for Dwight D. Eisenhower's "Atoms for Peace" initiative.

1963 - John Pennel set an indoor pole vault record in Memphis, Tennessee when he cleared 16 feet 3 inches.

1965 – NASA launched *Gemini 3*, the United States' first two-man space flight with Gus Grissom and John Young serving as the crew. It was reported that during this flight, Young became the first person to eat a corned-beef sandwich in space.

1971 - *The Concert for Bangladesh* documentary film of the benefit concert premiered in New York City.

1973 - *Concentration*, the longest-running game show in television to date came to an end after 15 years on NBC.

1981 - British great train robber Ronald Biggs was taken into custody in Barbados after his abduction from Brazil.

1982 - A military coup in Guatemala deposed the president and installed a junta led by Lt. Gen. Efrain Rios Montt.

1983 – United States President Ronald Reagan announced plans for a new space-based defense system called the Strategic Defense Initiative (SDI), later known as "Star Wars."

1985 - Musician, Billy Joel married model, Christie Brinkley in a private ceremony held in New York City. They divorced 9 years later.

Official logo for the Strategic Defense Initiative. Public domain.

1985 – "We Are the World," by USA for Africa, entered the *Billboard* music chart at #21.

1994 – Aeroflot Flight 593 crashed in Siberia when the pilot's fifteen-year old son accidentally disengaged the autopilot. All 75 people on board were killed.

1994 – A United States Air Force F-16 aircraft collided in mid-air with a C-130 at Pope Air Force Base. The crash hurled both aircraft back to the ground, destroyed several other aircraft and killed 24 United States Army soldiers. This later became known as the "Green Ramp Disaster."

A C-141 laying dormant following the Green Ramp Disaster. Photo from the U.S. Department of Defense. Public domain.

1996 - Lee Teng-hui was sworn in as Taiwan's first democratically elected President.

1998 - *Titanic* was the big winner at the *70th Academy Awards*, taking home 11 trophies.

2001 – The Russian *Mir* space station was disposed of by allowing it to fall from orbit, breaking up in the atmosphere before falling into the southern Pacific Ocean near Fiji.

2003 – Eleven soldiers of the 507th Maintenance Company as well as 18 U.S. Marines were killed in Nasiriyah, Iraq during the first major conflict of Operation Iraqi Freedom.

2005 – The United States 11th Circuit Court of Appeals, in a 2-1 decision, refused to order the reinsertion of Terri Schiavo's feeding tube.

2005 – A major explosion at BP's Texas City Refinery killed 15 workers.

2007 – The Iranian Navy seized Royal Navy personnel in the waters between Iran and Iraq.

MARCH 24th

BIRTHDAYS FOR MARCH 24th

1834 John Wesley Powell; geologist, explorer

1874 Harry Houdini; magician, escape artist

1887 Fatty (Roscoe) Arbuckle; actor

1898 Dorothy Stratton; Executive Director of Girl Scouts of America

1920 Gene Nelson; actor, dancer

1924 Norman Fell; actor

1930 Steve McQueen; actor

1934 William Smith; actor

1937 Bob Tillman; baseball

1940 Bob Mackie; fashion and costume designer

1944 R. Lee Ermey; American actor

1946 Lee Oskar; musician

1951 Pat Bradley; golf

1952 Tommy Hilfiger; designer

1953 Louie Anderson; American comedian

1954 Robert Carradine; actor, son of John Carradine

1954 Donna Pescow; actress

1956 Steve Ballmer; Microsoft CEO

1960 Kelly LeBrock; actress

1960 Barry Horowitz; American professional wrestler

1964 Annabella Sciorra; actress

1965 The Undertaker (Mark Callaway); American professional wrestler

1970 Lara Flynn Boyle; actress

1976 Peyton Manning; American football player

1982 Jack Swagger; American professional wrestler

EVENTS FOR MARCH 24th

1603 - Scottish King James VI became King James I of England.

1792 - Benjamin West had the honor of becoming the first American artist chosen to be President of the Royal Academy of London.

1832 – A group of men beat, tarred and feathered Mormon leader Joseph Smith, Jr. in Hiram, Ohio.

1878 – The British frigate HMS *Eurydice* sank, killing more than 300.

1882 – Robert Koch announced the discovery of mycobacterium tuberculosis, the bacterium responsible for tuberculosis.

1896 – Alexander Stepanovich Popov made the first radio signal transmission in history. He never applied for a patent on his invention.

1898 - The first United States automobile was sold. Mining engineer Robert Allison paid $1,000 for a Winton after seeing an advertisement in *Scientific American.*

1900 – Mayor of New York City Robert Anderson Van Wyck broke ground for a new underground "Rapid Transit Railroad" that would link Manhattan and Brooklyn. And thus was born the New York Subway.

1930 - The recently discovered 9th planet was given the name Pluto. Each member of the Lowell Observatory was allowed to vote on a short-list of three names: Minerva (which was already the name for an asteroid), Cronus (which had lost reputation through being proposed by the unpopular astronomer Thomas Jefferson Jackson See), and Pluto. The latter received every vote.

1934 - *Major Bowes' Amateur Hour* began airing on the NBC radio network and lasted for the next 17 years.

1936 – The longest game in NHL history to date was played between Detroit and Montreal. Detroit scored at 16:30 of the sixth overtime and won the game 1-0.

1944 – In an event later dramatized in the movie *The Great Escape*, 76 prisoners began breaking out of Stalag Luft III. Only three prisoners made it home.

The USS *Upshur* which transported Elvis Presley to join the 3rd Armored Division in Friedberg, Germany. Public domain.

1955 - Tennessee Williams's Southern drama, *Cat on a Hot Tin Roof*, staged by Elia Kazan, debuted on Broadway and received mixed reviews.

1958 – Elvis Presley reported to local draft board 86 in Memphis, Tennessee where he became Private Presley #53310761.

1965 – NASA spacecraft Ranger 9, equipped to convert its signals into a form suitable for showing on domestic television, delivered images of the Moon into ordinary homes before crash landing later that same day.

1987 – French Premier Jacques Chirac signed a contract with Walt Disney Productions for the creation of the Euro Disney theme park.

Main Street of Disneyland Paris. Copyrighted photo used by permission.

1989 - The United States' worst oil spill to date occurred as the supertanker Exxon Valdez ran aground on a reef in Alaska's Prince William Sound and began leaking 11 million gallons of crude.

1992 - Democrat Jerry Brown upset front-runner Bill Clinton in the Connecticut presidential primary.

1992 - A Chicago county circuit judge awarded a judgment against Milli Vanilli; a pop duo who admitted to lip-synching their parts. The judgment allowed for cash rebates of up to $3 to anyone proving they bought Milli Vanilli recordings prior to when the lip synching scandal began on November 27, 1990.

Astronaut Shannon Lucid exercising on a treadmill assembled in the Russian Mir space station Base Block module. Public domain.

1996 – Astronaut Shannon Lucid transferred from the space shuttle Atlantis to the Russian space station Mir, beginning a five-month stay.

1998 – Mitchell Johnson and Andrew Golden, aged 11 and 13 respectively, fired upon teachers and students at Westside Middle School in Jonesboro, Arkansas; five people were killed and ten were wounded.

1998 – A tornado swept through Dantan, India killing 250 people and injuring 3000 others.

1999 – NATO commenced air bombardment against Yugoslavia, marking the first time NATO has attacked a sovereign country.

2000 – S&P 500 index reached an intraday high of 1,552.87, a peak that, due to the collapse of the dot-com bubble, it would not reach again for another seven-and-a-half years.

2001 - Apple Inc. presented the initial release of the Mac OS X Operating System.

2003 – The Arab League voted 21-1 in favor of a resolution demanding the immediate and unconditional removal of U.S. and British soldiers from Iraq.

2006 – Long-term election protests in Belarus are broken by police.

2008 – Bhutan officially becomes a democracy, with its first ever general election.

2009 – *Ward's Daily Almanac* began as a two-minute daily feature for radio stations. The first broadcast of this program was heard on WBNL in Indiana.

Ralph Turpen, Owner and General Manager of WBNL. Photo used by permission.

MARCH 25th

BIRTHDAYS FOR MARCH 25th

1867 Arturo Toscanini; conductor, cellist

1881 Bela Bartok; composer

1901 Ed Begley, Sr.; actor

1911 Jack Ruby; killer of Lee Harvey Oswald

1918 Howard Cosell (Cohen); sportscaster

1921 Nancy Kelly; actress

1922 Eileen Ford; Ford Model Agency Founder

1925 (Mary) Flannery O'Connor; writer

1928 James Lovell, Jr.; astronaut

1932 Gene Shalit; American film critic

1932 Woody Held; baseball

1934 Gloria Steinem; Writer, feminist

1934 Johnny Burnette; singer

1937 Tom Monaghan; founder of Dominos pizza

1938 Hoyt Axton; singer, musician, songwriter

1940 Anita Bryant; singer

1942 Aretha Franklin; Grammy Award-winning singer, Rock and Roll Hall of Famer

1943 Paul Michael Glaser; actor, director

1947 Elton John (Reginald Kenneth Dwight); musician, singer, songwriter

1961 John Stockwell; actor

1965 Sarah Jessica Parker; actress

1966 Jeff Healey; musician, guitarist, singer, songwriter

1966 Tom Glavine; baseball

1967 Debi Thomas; figure skater

1971 Cammi Granato; hockey, 1998 Olympic team

1971 Sheryl Swoopes; basketball, US Olympic team

EVENTS FOR MARCH 25th

1409 - The Council of Pisa formed to try to resolve the schism in the Catholic Church between the popes Gregory and Benedict.

1584 – Sir Walter Raleigh is granted a patent (or charter) to colonize Virginia.

1634 – The first colonists to Maryland arrived at St. Clement's Island on Maryland's western shore and founded the settlement of St. Mary's.

1807 - The Slave Trade Act became law and thus the slave trade in England was abolished.

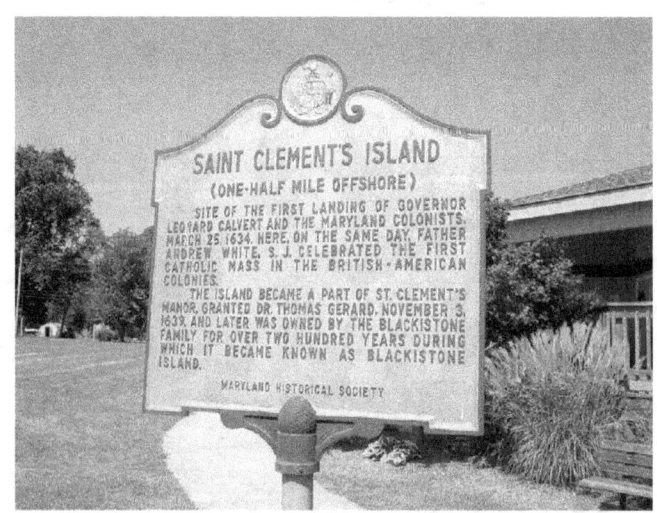

St. Clement's Island Historic Marker. Public domain.

1807 – The Swansea and Mumbles Railway, then known as the Oystermouth Railway, becomes the first passenger carrying railway in the world.

Before becoming motorized, early railroad cars were pulled by a horse. Public domain.

1811 – Percy Bysshe Shelley was expelled from the University of Oxford for publishing the pamphlet *The Necessity of Atheism*.

1931 – A group of nine men, known as "The Scottsboro Boys" were arrested in Alabama and charged with the rape of two women.

The former Presidential Yacht USS *Sequoia* on the Potomac River near Washington D.C. Public domain.

1932 – The motion picture *Tarzan the Ape Man* opened with Olympic gold medal swimmer Johnny Weismuller in the title role.

1933 – President Herbert Hoover accepted the newly commissioned USS *Sequoia* as the official presidential yacht. Forty-four years later, at President Carter's direction, the U.S. government sold it at auction in Manalapan, Florida for $270,000, as a symbolic cutback in Federal Government spending (annual cost to the U.S. Navy was $800,000) and to help eliminate signs of an "imperial presidency."

1941 – Yugoslavia joined the Tripartite Pact, a military alliance directed against the United States and Britain.

1941 - The first paprika mill (Carolina Paprika Mills, Inc.) was incorporated in Dollon, South Carolina.

1943 - Jimmy Durante and Garry Moore finished out the season for *The Abbott and Costello Show* when Lou Costello became ill.

Children waving German, Italian, and Japanese flags of 1938 in a Japanese propaganda poster for the Tripartite Pact. The translation of the Japanese headline: Good friends in three countries. Public domain.

1946 - The Soviet Union announced that its troops in Iran would be withdrawn within six weeks. The Iranian crisis was one of the first tests of power between the United States and the Soviet Union in the postwar era.

1948 – The first successful tornado forecast predicted that a tornado would strike Tinker Air Force Base, Oklahoma. It did.

1954 - RCA began commercially producing television sets equipped to receive programs in color. Initially the price tag for a set was $1,000 but the price was cut to $495 by August.

1957 - The Treaty of Rome was signed, providing for the establishment on January 1, 1958 of the Common Market in Europe. The countries that signed were Belgium, France, Italy, Luxembourg, the Netherlands, and West Germany.

1969 – During their honeymoon, John Lennon and Yoko Ono held their first "Bed-In for Peace" at the Amsterdam Hilton Hotel (room #902). Their stunt lasted until March 31st.

1979 – The first fully functional space shuttle orbiter, Columbia, was delivered to the John F. Kennedy Space Center to be prepared for its first launch.

Columbia on the launch pad waiting to be launched on its first mission. Pubic domain.

1980 - Archbishop Robert Runcie was enthroned as Archbishop of Canterbury.

1982 - The television show *Cagney and Lacey*, starring Tyne Daly and Sharon Gless, debuted on CBS.

1988 - Former nuclear technician Mordechai Vanunu was found guilty in an Israeli court of treason for revealing Israel's nuclear secrets.

1988 – "The Candle Demonstration" in Bratislava was the first mass demonstration of the 1980s against the communist regime in Czechoslovakia.

1990 - Carbon monoxide and cyanide caused 87 deaths from smoke inhalation during a fire at the Happy Land Social Club in New York.

1994 - Neo-Nazis firebombed a synagogue in the north German town of Luebeck; the first such incident in Germany since the end of the Second World War. The synagogue's cantor was a Holocaust survivor. He and five other people living in the four-story building escaped.

1994 - At the end of a 15-month mission, the last U.S. troops departed Somalia, leaving 20,000 U.N. troops behind to keep the peace and facilitate "nation building" in the divided country.

1995 - Former heavyweight boxing champion Mike Tyson was freed from an Indiana prison three years after his conviction for rape.

1996 – An 81-day long standoff between the anti-government group, Montana Freemen, and law enforcement began near Jordan, Montana.

1996 - Officials from the 15 European Union states agreed to recommend a ban on exports of British beef products because of concern over mad cow disease.

1996 - France, Britain and the United States signed the South Pacific Nuclear Free Zone Treaty that banned the use, testing, and possession of nuclear weapons within the borders of the zone. The zone was defined as south of the Equator, north of the 60th parallel south (the northern limit of the Antarctic

Treaty zone), east of the 115th meridian east, and west of the 115th meridian west (the western limit of the Treaty of Tlatelolco Latin American Nuclear-Weapon-Free Zone).

1996 - Abel Goodman, the world's first patient to receive a permanent electric heart, died in Britain after having lived with his implant for six months.

2006 – A gunman killed six people before taking his own life at a party in Seattle's Capitol Hill neighborhood.

2006 – Protesters demanding a new election in Belarus, following the rigged Belarusian presidential election in 2006, clashed with riot police. Opposition leader Aleksander Kozulin was among several protesters arrested.

MARCH 26th

BIRTHDAYS FOR MARCH 26th

1773 Nathaniel Bowditch; astronomer, author

1874 Robert Frost; Pulitzer prize-winning poet

1880 Duncan Hines; author, traveler, pioneer of restaurant ratings for travelers

1911 Tennessee Williams; Pulitzer prize-winning playwright

1914 William Westmoreland; U.S. Army General

1916 Sterling Hayden; actor

1919 Strother Martin; actor

1921 Joe Loco; jazz musician, arranger

1923 Bob Elliott; comedian

1925 Pierre Boulez; conductor, composer

1929 Tom Foley; American politician, former Speaker of the House

1929 Maurice Simon; jazz musician, tenor saxophonist

1930 Sandra Day O'Connor; U.S. Supreme Court Justice

1931 Leonard Nimoy; actor, director

1932 Dick Nolan; football

1934 Gino Cappelletti; football

1934 Alan Arkin; actor

1937 Wayne "The Wall" Embry; basketball

1940 James Caan; actor

1940 Nancy Pelosi; American politician and 60th Speaker of the House

1940 Braulio Baeza; National Horse Racing Hall of Famer, jockey

1942 Erica Jong; writer

1943 Bob Woodward; investigative reporter

1944 Diana Ross; singer, actress

1947 Dar Robinson; American stuntman

1948 Richard Tandy; musician

1948 Steven Tyler (Tallarico); singer

1949 Vicki Lawrence; Emmy Award-winning actress

1949 Fran Sheehan; musician, bassist

1950 Teddy Pendergrass; singer

1950 Martin Short; actor

1953 Lincoln Chafee; Rhode Island Senator

1954 Curtis Sliwa; Guardian Angels Founder

1956 Charly McClain; American singer

1957 Leeza Gibbons; TV hostess

1960 Jennifer Grey; actress

1960 Marcus Allen; football

1962 John Stockton; basketball

1968 Kenny Chesney; singer

1973 Lawrence E. Page; co-founder of Google

1973 T.R. Knight; American actor

1985 Keira Knightley; English actress

EVENTS FOR MARCH 26th

1026 - Conrad II was crowned Holy Roman Emperor by Pope John XIX.

1828 - Austrian composer Franz Schubert gave his one and only public concert.

1830 – *The Wayne Sentinel* in Palmyra, New York featured an ad announcing that *The Book Of Mormon* was "for sale, wholesale and retail, at the Palmyra Bookstore."

1885 - George Eastman manufactured the first commercial motion-picture film at his factory in Rochester, New York.

1913 - The Bulgarians took Adrianople in the Balkan War.

1917 - At the start of the battle of Gaza, the British cavalry under Murray withdrew when 17,000 Turks blocked their advance.

1918 – In World War I, French Marshal Ferdinand Foch was appointed Supreme Commander of the Allied armies on the western front.

1923 - Sarah Bernhardt died.

1934 – The first driving test was introduced in the United Kingdom.

Ferdinand Foch. Public domain.

1937 - Joe DiMaggio took Ty Cobb's advice and replaced his 40-ounce bat with a 36-ounce bat.

Crystal City's tribute to Popeye. Public domain.

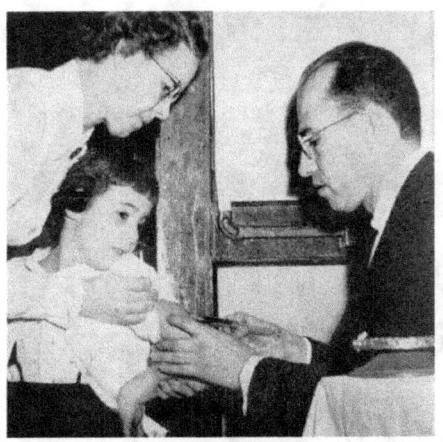

Magazine photo of Jonas Salk in laboratory, taken by Yousuf Karsh specifically for *Wisdom Magazine*. Public domain.

1937 – Crystal City, Texas, erected America's first monument to a comic strip hero. The six-foot-tall, brightly colored concrete statue of Popeye was unveiled in Popeye Park during the city's second annual Spinach Festival.

1945 - The Battle of Iwo Jima came to an end.

1951 - The United States Air Force Flag, which features a coat of arms, 13 white stars and the Air Force Seal on a blue background, was approved.

1953 – Dr. Jonas Salk announced a new vaccine. It was a vaccine to prevent poliomyelitis, more commonly known as polio.

1964 - Stephen Edward Clark set the fastest speed record ever noted by an American swimmer when, at the Yale University pool, he was timed at 4.89 miles-per-hour.

1967 – Ten thousand people gathered for one of many Central Park "be-ins" in New York City. A "be-in" was a way of protesting against various issues such as US involvement in the Vietnam War and racism. The gathering on this date was to protest the war.

1969 - *The ABC Movie of the Week* featured the pilot for *Marcus Welby, M.D.* with ratings so high it became a long-running series starring Robert Young.

1971 - William Conrad starred as *Cannon* on CBS-TV in a one-time television event that became a series that year.

1971 - Sheikh Mujibur Rahman declared East Pakistan the independent republic of Bangladesh.

1973 - Women were allowed on to the floor of the London Stock Exchange for the first time.

1973 - *The Young and the Restless* debuted on CBS.

1975 - *Tommy*, the film based on The Who's rock opera, premiered in London.

1976 – Queen Elizabeth II sent the first royal email, from the Royal Signals and Radar Establishment.

1979 – In a ceremony at the White House, President Sadat of Egypt and Prime Minister Begin of Israel signed a peace treaty.

Egyptian President Anwar Sadat and Israeli Prime Minister Menachem Begin acknowledge applause during a joint session of Congress in Washington, D.C. Photo provided by the U.S. Library of Congress.

1981 - Comedienne Carol Burnett won a $1.6 million libel suit against *The National Enquirer*. The amount was later reduced to $800,000 on appeal.

1982 – A groundbreaking ceremony for the Vietnam Veterans Memorial was held in Washington, D.C.

Various items are left at the wall by loved ones in tribute to their fallen. Photo by Kelvin Kay. Used by permission.

1990 - Halston, born Roy Halston Frowick, a leading designer of women's clothes in the 70s, died at age 57.

1996 - The International Monetary Fund approved a $10.2 billion loan for Russia to help the country further transform its economy.

1997 - The bodies of 39 members of the Heaven's Gate cult were found after killing themselves in a mass suicide.

1999 – The "Melissa worm" infected Microsoft word processing and e-mail systems around the world.

1999 – A jury in Michigan found Dr. Jack Kevorkian guilty of second-degree murder for administering a lethal injection to a terminally ill man.

2005 – The Taiwanese government called on one million Taiwanese to demonstrate in Taipei, in opposition to the Anti-Secession Law of the People's Republic of China. Around 200,000 to 300,000 attended the walk.

2006 – In Scotland, the prohibition of smoking in all substantially enclosed public places went into force.

2006 – The military junta ruling Burma officially named Naypyidaw, a new city in Mandalay Division, as the new capital. Yangon had formerly been the nation's capital.

BIRTHDAYS FOR MARCH 27th

1785 King Louis XVII of France

1813 Nathaniel Currier; illustrator

1868 Patty Smith Hill; songwriter, co-writer of "Happy Birthday to You"

1899 Gloria Swanson; actress

1901 Carl Barks; Disney animator, cartoonist

1914 Richard Denning; actor

1914 Snooky Lanson (Roy Landman); singer

1920 Richard Hayman; musician, harmonica player, conductor

1921 Harold Nicholas; dancer

1931 David Janssen; actor

1939 William Caleb (Cale) Yarborough; auto racer

1942 Michael York; actor

1950 Tony Banks; musician, keyboardist

1950 Vic Harris; baseball

1951 Bobby Lalonde; hockey

1952 Maria Schneider; actress

1953 Annemarie Moser-Pröll; skier

1959 Andrew Farriss; musician, keyboardist

1963 Quentin Tarantino; Academy Award-winning screenwriter

1963 Xuxa; Brazilian television personality

1963 Randall Cunningham; football

1970 Mariah Carey; Grammy Award-winning singer

1972 Charlie Haas; professional wrestler

1975 Fergie; American pop singer

EVENTS FOR MARCH 27th

1625 - Charles I, King of England, Scotland and Ireland, ascends to throne.

1794 – The United States Government established a permanent navy and authorized the building of six frigates.

1836 – The first Mormon temple dedicated in Kirtland, Ohio. The dedication service, led by Joseph Smith Jr., is said to have lasted 8 hours.

1841 – The first Steam Fire Engine ever built in the United States was tested in New York City. The steam engine was approved by authorities but, ironically, it was initially rejected by firefighters who felt they were being replaced.

The first American-built Steam Fire Engine. Built by Paul Rapsey Hodge. Public domain.

1851 – First reported sighting of the Yosemite Valley by Europeans.

1855 - Abraham Gesner received patent #12,612 for kerosene.

1881 – Rioting took place in Basingstoke, England in protest against the daily promotion of rigid Temperance by the Salvation Army.

1905 - The use of fingerprints was used to solve the murders of Thomas and Ann Farrow, a pair of London shopkeepers. This was the first known use of fingerprints to solve a murder case.

1912 - Helen Taft, wife of President William Taft, and the Viscountess Chinda, wife of the Japanese ambassador, planted two Yoshina cherry trees on the northern bank of the Potomac River, near the Jefferson Memorial. The event was held in celebration of a gift of 3,020 cherry trees from the Japanese government to the U.S. Government.

1931 – British writer Arnold Bennett died of typhoid in London shortly after returning from a visit to Paris, where he drank local water to prove it was safe. He was incorrect.

1933 - Japan announced it would leave the League of Nations citing a diplomatic disadvantage due to inferior powers.

1933 - The Farm Credit Administration was authorized by Executive Order 6084.

1941 - Prince Paul of Yugoslavia was deposed in a coup d'etat following his pact with Adolf Hitler.

1945 - Ella Fitzgerald and the Delta Rhythm Boys recorded "It's Only a Paper Moon".

1945 – Germany launched its last V2 rocket from the Hague in the Netherlands, crashing in Orpington, southeast of London. The last person known to be killed by this rocket was 34-year old Ivy Millichamp.

1945 - Vital water routes and ports of Japan were mined by air in order to disrupt enemy shipping. This marked the beginning of "Operation Starvation."

1952 - Sun Records of Memphis, Tennessee began operations. Among others, artists who made their first recordings there included Carl Perkins, Roy Orbison, Johnny Cash, and Elvis Presley.

1955 - Steve McQueen made his network television debut as a guest star in the episode "The Chivington Raid" on *The Goodyear Television Playhouse*.

1958 - Nikita Khrushchev became Soviet premier and first secretary of the Communist Party.

1964 – "The Good Friday Earthquake," the most powerful American earthquake to date at a magnitude of 9.2, struck South Central Alaska, killed 125 people and caused massive damage to the city of Anchorage.

Looking along 4th street in Anchorage after the Good Friday Earthquake. Public domain.

1968 - Yuri Gagarin, the first man who was launched into space in 1961, was killed in a plane crash near Moscow.

1972 - Tom Batiuk launched his comic strip *Funky Winkerbean*.

1975 – Construction began on the Trans-Alaska Pipeline System.

1977 - Two Boeing 747 airliners collided on a foggy runway on Tenerife in the Canary Islands, killing 583 (all 248 on KLM and 335 on Pan Am). Sixty-one survived on the Pan Am flight.

1980 – The Norwegian oil platform Alexander L. Kielland collapsed in the North Sea, 123 of its crew of 212 were lost in the tragedy.

1980 - Mount St. Helens in Washington State became active after 123 years. Less than a month later the volcano erupted and killed 57 people, nearly 7,000 big game animals (deer, elk, and bear), and an estimated 12 million fish from a hatchery. It destroyed or extensively damaged over 200 homes, 185 miles of highway and 15 miles of railways.

1980 – A steep fall in silver prices, resulting from the Hunt Brothers attempting to corner the market in silver, led to panic on commodity and futures exchanges.

1982 – Harriet Stratemeyer Adams, one of the authors of the *Nancy Drew* series, died at age 89 of a heart attack.

1985 - Billy Dee Williams was given a star on the Hollywood Walk of Fame. His star was placed between Joan Davis and Harry Carey at 1521 Vine Street.

1990 – The United States began broadcasting TV Martí to Cuba in an effort to bridge the information blackout imposed by the Castro regime.

1996 - Yigal Amir received a life sentence for assassinating Israeli Prime Minister Yitzhak Rabin in November 1995.

1998 – The Food and Drug Administration approved Viagra for use as a treatment for male impotence, the first pill to be approved for this condition in the United States.

1999 – An F-117 Nighthawk was shot down during the Kosovo War, the only one to be lost in combat.

A US Air Force F-117A Nighthawk Stealth Fighter aircraft flies over Nellis Air Force Base, Nevada. Public domain.

2000 – A Phillips Petroleum plant exploded in Pasadena, Texas; one person was killed and 71 were injured.

2002 – A Palestinian suicide bomber killed 29 people partaking of the Passover meal in Netanya, Israel.

2004 – HMS *Scylla*, a decommissioned Leander class frigate, was sunk as an artificial reef off Cornwall, the first of its kind in Europe.

2009 – The dam holding back Situ Gintung, an artificial lake in Indonesia, failed and killed at least 99 people.

BIRTHDAYS FOR MARCH 28th

1811 Saint John Neumann; first male saint of America

1895 Christian Herter; 59th Governor of Massachusetts

1899 August Busch; beer magnate, St. Louis Cardinals owner

1903 Rudolf Serkin; concert pianist

1905 Marlin Perkins; American naturalist and television host

1907 "Swifty" Lazar; American talent agent

1914 Edmund Muskie; U.S. Senator, Secretary of State

1933 Frank Hughes Murkowski; U.S. Senator

1944 Ken Howard; actor

1947 John Landecker; American disk jockey

1948 Gerry House; American radio personality

1948 John Evan; British musician (Jethro Tull)

1948 Sam Lacey; basketball

1948 Dianne Wiest; Academy Award-winning actress

1948 Milan Williams; musician, keyboardist, drummer, trombonist, guitarist

1949 Ronnie Ray Smith; Olympic gold medalist, sprinter

1955 Reba (Nell) McEntire; singer

1958 Curt Hennig; American professional wrestler

1961 Byron Scott; basketball

1964 Salt (Cheryl James); Grammy Award-winning rap singer

1969 Rodney Atkins; American country music singer-songwriter

1981 Julia Stiles; actress

EVENTS FOR MARCH 28th

1797 - Nathaniel Briggs of New Hampshire patented the washing machine.

1834 – The United States Senate censured President Andrew Jackson for his actions in de-funding the Second Bank of the United States.

1854 - Britain and France declared war on Russia in the Crimean War.

1885 – After the London organization had been formed 20 years earlier, the United States Salvation Army was officially organized.

1891 - In London, the first world championship for amateur weightlifters was held.

1910 – Henri Fabre became the first person to fly a seaplane, the Fabre Hydravion, after taking off from a water runway near Martigues, France.

Henri Fabre taking off on the world's first seaplane. Public domain.

1920 – The Palm Sunday

tornado outbreak of 1920 affected the Great Lakes region and Deep South states. At least 38 tornadoes were reported.

1922 - Bradley A. Fiske, of Washington, D.C., patented a device to read microfilm.

1930 - The cities of Constantinople and Angora changed their names to Istanbul and Ankara, Turkey respectively.

1933 - The German Reichstag conferred dictatorial powers to Adolph Hitler.

1941 - In World War II the Italian navy was defeated in the Battle of Cape Matapan.

1941 - British novelist and essayist Virginia Woolf committed suicide at age 59. Battling depression, Woolf put on her overcoat, filled its pockets with stones, and walked into the River Ouse near her home and drowned.

1963 - Sonny Werblin announced the New York Titans of the American Football League had changed its name to become the New York Jets.

1964 – Wax likenesses of The Beatles were put on display in London's Madame Tussaud's Wax Museum. The Beatles were the first pop stars to be displayed at the museum.

1968 – Brazilian high school student Edson Luís de Lima Souto was shot by the police in a protest for cheaper meals at a restaurant for low-income students. The aftermath of his death is one of the first major events against the military dictatorship.

1969 – The McGill français protest occurred. It was the second largest protest in Montreal's history with 10,000 trade unionists, leftist activists, CEGEP students, and even some McGill students at McGill's Roddick Gates. This led to the majority of the protesters getting arrested.

1978 – The US Supreme Court handed down 5-3 decision in *Stump v. Sparkman*, 435 U.S. 349, a controversial case involving involuntary sterilization and judicial immunity. This action stemmed from a case in 1971 when Judge Harold D. Stump granted a mother's petition to have a tubal ligation performed on her 15-year-old daughter, whom the mother alleged was "somewhat retarded."

1979 – In Pennsylvania, operators failed to recognize that a relief valve was stuck open in the primary coolant system of Three Mile Island's Unit 2 nuclear reactor following an unexpected shutdown. As a result, enough coolant drained out of the system to allow the core to overheat and partially melt down.

The Three Mile Island nuclear generating station, which suffered a partial meltdown in 1979. The reactors are in the smaller domes with rounded tops (the large smokestacks are just cooling towers).

1984 - Bob Irsay, owner of the Baltimore Colts, moved the team to Indianapolis.

1984 - British Cultural Attache and British Council representative Kenneth Whitty was assassinated on an Athens street in Greece by a single gunman. The assassination coincided with the start of a European tour of the play, *A School For Scandal*, to celebrate the British Councils 50th anniversary. The play opened in Athens three days later on March 31st.

1985 - Devan Nair resigned as president of Singapore on health grounds, but some attributed his resignation to alcoholism.

1986 - More than 6,000 radio stations around the world played "We are the World," simultaneously, at 10:15 a.m. EST.

1990 – President George H. W. Bush posthumously awarded Jesse Owens the Congressional Gold Medal.

1994 – Twelve-year-old schoolgirl Nikki Conroy was stabbed to death at Hall Garth School in Middlesbrough, England after an armed man walked into her math classroom and attacked pupils with a knife. Stephen James Wilkinson was later convicted of manslaughter on the grounds of diminished responsibility.

1996 – Israel's inquiry into the assassination of Yitzhak Rabin concluded security agencies ignored intelligence information that a Jewish militant might try to kill the prime minister.

1998 - Lucy Lawless, the athletic beauty of television's syndicated *Xena: Warrior Princess* married Rob Tapert.

2000 – A Murray County, Georgia, school bus was hit by a CSX freight train (3 children died in this accident).

2003 – In a "friendly fire" incident, two A-10 *Thunderbolt II*s (attack aircraft from the United States Idaho Air National Guard's 190th Fighter Squadron) attacked

An A-10 Thunderbolt II in flight. Public domain.

British tanks participating in the 2003 invasion of Iraq, killing British soldier Matty Hull.

2005 – The 2005 Sumatran earthquake rocked Indonesia, and at magnitude 8.7 was the second strongest earthquake since 1965.

2006 – At least one million union members, students and unemployed took to the streets in France in protest of the government's proposed First Employment Contract law.

BIRTHDAYS FOR MARCH 29th

1790 John Tyler; 10th U.S. President

1867 Cy Young; baseball

1874 Lou Hoover (Henry); U.S. First Lady

1916 Eugene McCarthy; U.S. Senator

1917 Man o' War; American thoroughbred racehorse

1918 Sam Walton; American businessman

1918 Pearl Mae Bailey; jazz singer

1927 John McLaughlin; TV host, editor, columnist

1937 Billy Carter; brother of U.S. President Jimmy Carter

1943 Eric Idle; actor

1943 Sir John Major; former British Prime Minister

1943 Vangelis; Greek musician and composer

1944 Terry Jacks; Canadian musician, songwriter, and activist

1945 Walt (Clyde) Frazier; Basketball Hall of Famer

1947 Bobby Kimball; singer

1956 Kurt Thomas; gymnast

1957 Christopher Lambert; actor

1959 Perry Farrell (Simon Bernstein); musician

1964 Elle Macpherson; model, actress

1968 Lucy Lawless; actress

1971 Robert Gibbs; American White House press secretary for President Barack Obama

1976 Jennifer Capriati; Olympic gold-medalist tennis

EVENTS FOR MARCH 29th

1549 – The city of Salvador da Bahia, the first capital of Brazil, was founded.

1638 – Swedish colonists established the first settlement in Delaware, and named it New Sweden.

1806 - The Great National Pike, also known as the Cumberland Road, became the first highway funded by the national treasury.

1848 - For the first time in recorded history, Niagara Falls ceased flowing when an ice jam in the river above the rim of the falls caused the water to stop moving.

1867 - The British North America Act established the Dominion of Canada comprising Quebec, Ontario, Nova Scotia and New Brunswick.

1871 – Queen Victoria opened the Royal Albert Hall in London in memory of her late consort Prince Albert.

The grand opening of the Royal Albert Hall in London by Queen Victoria as illustrated in *The Graphic*, an illustrated newspaper of the time. Public domain.

1882 - Connecticut granted a charter to the Knights of Columbus.

1886 – Dr. John Pemberton brews the first batch of Coca-Cola in a backyard in Atlanta, Georgia.

1903 - *The Times* in London became the first newspaper to establish an ongoing arrangement with the Marconi Telegraph Company for the regular transmission of news between the United States and the UK.

1912 - English Antarctic explorer Robert Falcon Scott died as his expedition attempted to return home after reaching the South Pole.

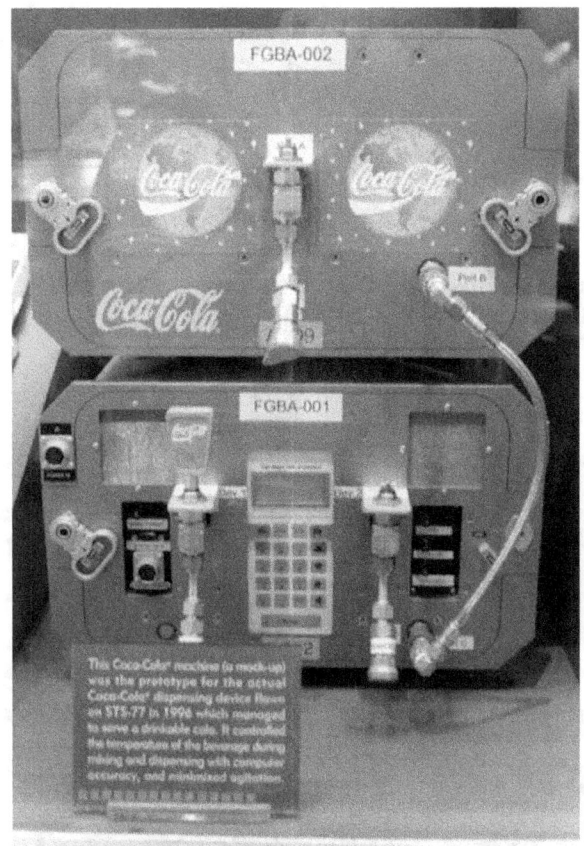

Coca-Cola has come a long way since Dr. Pemberton's 1886 brew. This is a mock-up of the Coke dispenser that was launched aboard the Space Shuttle Endeavour in 1996. Used by permission.

1929 - President Herbert Hoover had a phone installed at his desk in the Oval Office of the White House. Telephones and a telephone switchboard had been in use at the White House since 1878, when President Rutherford B. Hayes had the first one installed, but no phone had ever been installed at the president's desk until Hoover's administration.

1932 - Comedian Jack Benny appeared on radio for the first time during his appearance on Ed Sullivan's *Broadway's Greatest*.

1936 - Nazi propaganda claimed that 98.76 percent of the German population voted for Adolph Hitler. All other ballots were deemed as void.

1939 - Actor Clark Gable married actress-comedienne Carole Lombard on this date in Kingman, Arizona.

1945 – During World War II, this marked the last day of the V-1 flying bomb attacks on England. This flying German missile could be described as an early cruise missile.

A German crew rolling out their V-1. Photo from the German Federal Archive.

1951 - *The King and I*, a Rodgers and Hammerstein production, opened on Broadway at the St. James Theatre. It would play there for over three years presenting 1,246 performances.

1961 - The United States constitution was amended to give residents of the District of Columbia the right to vote in presidential elections.

1962 - Jack Paar left *The Tonight Show*, leaving a salary of $250,000 and an audience of eight million people. Johnny Carson would later replace him.

1967 - The first nationwide strike in the 30-year life of the American Federation of Television and Radio Artists (AFTRA) began. It would last for 13 days.

1971 – Lt. William Calley was convicted of premeditated murder and was later sentenced to life in prison for his part in the My Lai Massacre.

MANSON, Charles Milles

CII 966 856

Manson's mug shot taken when he was booked into the San Quentin Correctional Center in January of 1971. Public domain.

1971 – A Los Angeles, California jury recommended the death penalty for Charles Manson and three female followers.

1973 - After recording "The Cover of the Rolling Stone," Dr. Hook made the front of the cultural magazine. The magazine, however, decided that instead of a photograph, they would use a caricature.

1973 - Two months after the signing of the Vietnam peace agreement, the last U.S. combat troops left South Vietnam as Hanoi freed the remaining American prisoners of war held in North Vietnam.

1974 - The first close-up pictures of the planet Mercury were taken by the United States spacecraft Mariner 10.

1982 - The oldest soap opera on television *Search for Tomorrow* jumped from CBS, where it started 30 years ago, to NBC.

1987 - It took Hulk Hogan 11 minutes, and 43 seconds to pin Andre the Giant in front of 93,136 *Wrestlemania III* fans at the Silverdome in Pontiac, Michigan. At the time, the event set the world indoor attendance record.

1990 - The major music-producing companies agreed on this date to put a warning label on recordings that contained potentially offensive lyrics.

1994 – Guatemala's government and leftist rebels signed a breakthrough human rights accord that boosted hopes of ending 33 years of civil war.

1999 – The Dow Jones Industrial Average closed above the 10,000 mark (10,006.78) for the first time ever, during the height of the Internet boom.

2004 – Bulgaria, Estonia, Latvia, Lithuania, Romania, Slovakia and Slovenia joined NATO as full members.

2004 – The Republic of Ireland became the first country in the world to ban smoking in all work places, including bars and restaurants.

2008 – Thirty-five countries and over 370 cities joined Earth Hour for the first time. During Earth Hour, held annually on the last Saturday of March, households and businesses are asked to turn off their non-essential lights and other electrical appliances for one hour to raise awareness towards the need to take action on climate change.

2010 – Two female suicide bombers hit the Moscow Metro system at the peak of the morning rush hour. At least 40 people were killed, and over 100 injured.

BIRTHDAYS FOR MARCH 30th

1750 John Stafford Smith; English composer

1853 Vincent van Gogh; artist

1913 Frankie Laine (LoVecchio); singer

1919 McGeorge Bundy; Ford Foundation President

1927 Peter Marshall (Pierre LaCock); TV host

1929 Richard Dysart; actor

1930 John Astin; actor

1937 Warren Beatty; actor

1940 Jerry Lucas; Basketball Hall of Famer, Olympic Gold Medalist

1941 Robert C. Smith; U.S. Senator

1942 Graeme Edge; musician, drummer

1945 Eric Clapton; musician, guitarist, singer, songwriter

1950 LaRue Martin; basketball

1957 Paul Reiser; actor

1963 MC Hammer (Stanley Kirk Burrell); rap singer

1964 Tracy Chapman; folksinger, songwriter

1964 Ian Ziering; actor

1965 Piers Morgan; British journalist

1968 Celine Dion; singer, Grammy winner

1970 Secretariat; American racehorse

1979 Norah Jones; American singer and pianist

EVENTS FOR MARCH 30th

1806 - Joseph Bonaparte, brother of Napoleon, was proclaimed King of Naples.

1814 - Britain and its allies against Napoleon Bonaparte marched in triumph into Paris.

1822 – The Florida Territory was created in the United States.

1842 – Anesthesia was used for the first time, in an operation by Dr. Crawford Long. The anesthetic used was ether and was utilized when Dr. Long removed a tumor from James Venable.

1855 - In territorial Kansas' first election, some 5,000 so-called "Border Ruffians" invaded the territory from western Missouri and forced the election of a pro-slavery legislature. Even though the number of votes cast exceeded the number of eligible voters in the territory, Kansas Governor Andrew Reeder reluctantly approved the election to prevent further bloodshed.

1856 - The Treaty of Paris was signed, ending the Crimean War and guaranteeing the integrity of Ottoman Turkey.

1858 – Hyman L. Lipman, of Philadelphia, Pennsylvania, patented the pencil, which did have an attached eraser.

1863 - William, Prince of Denmark, was recognized as king of Greece and took the title George I.

1867 – Russia sold Alaska to the United States for two-cents an acre.

The original check used to pay for Alaska, worth $7.2 million. Public domain.

1870 - United States Congress readmitted Texas to the Union after it had seceded in 1861 to join the Confederate States.

Luftwaffe propaganda photo. Public domain.

1923 - In New York, the Audubon Ballroom was the site of the first dance marathon. The marathon began at 6:57pm and lasted until the next evening at 9:57pm, and was won by Alma Cummings who wore out six dance partners in the process.

1939 – The Heinkel He 100 fighter, a German pre-World War II fighter aircraft, set a world airspeed record of 463 mph with test pilot Hans Dieterle at the controls.

1945 - The Baltic Sea port of Danzig, or Gdansk, was captured by the Russians.

1954 – The Yonge Street subway line opened in Toronto and became the first subway in Canada.

1964 - *Jeopardy* first aired on NBC-TV. Host, Art Fleming never missed a show in 2,500 programs.

1970 - Secretariat, who would win horse racing's Triple Crown in 1973, was born at Meadow Farm in Caroline County, Virginia.

1974 - John Denver experienced his first #1 hit with "Sunshine on My Shoulders."

1978 - One of the most widely remembered episodes of *The Waltons* was broadcast. This episode, "Grandma Comes Home," was the sixth season finale because Ellen Corby, who played the role of "Grandma Walton," returned after suffering a stroke in 1977; and this was the last episode in which Will Geer, who played the role of "Grandpa Walton," appeared because he died on April 22, 1978 of respiratory failure at the age of 76.

1979 - Airey Neave, opposition Conservative spokesman on Northern Ireland, died when a bomb exploded in his car in the House of Commons car park.

1979 - In a two-day referendum, the people of Iran voted overwhelmingly in favor of establishing an Islamic Republic.

1981 – While leaving a speaking engagement at the Washington Hilton Hotel in Washington, D.C., President Reagan and three others were shot and wounded by John Hinckley, Jr. Reagan suffered a punctured lung, but prompt medical attention allowed him to recover quickly. Hinckley was later found not guilty by reason of insanity and was confined to a psychiatric facility

1994 - French Prime Minister Edouard Balladur formally scrapped a discredited youth wage law, which had sparked nationwide street protests.

2006 – The United Kingdom Terrorism Act 2006 became law.

MARCH 31st

BIRTHDAYS FOR MARCH 31st

1596 Rene Descartes; philosopher

1685 Johann Sebastian Bach; German composer

1732 Franz Joseph Haydn; composer

1878 Jack Johnson; heavyweight boxing champion

1927 Cesar Chavez; labor leader

1928 Gordie (Gordon) Howe; Hockey Hall of Famer

1928 Lefty (William Orville) Frizzell; Country Music Hall of Famer

1929 Liz Claiborne; fashion designer

1934 Shirley Jones; singer, actress

1934 Richard Chamberlain; American actor

1935 Herb Alpert; bandleader, record company executive

1938 Arthur B. Rubinstein; American composer

1940 Barney Frank; American politician

1940 Patrick Leahy; American politician

1942 Michael Savage (Michael Weiner); American radio host and political commentator

1943 Christopher Walken; American actor

1944 Mick Ralphs; musician, guitarist

1944 Angus King, Jr.; 72nd Governor of Maine

1945 Valerie Curtin; American actress, writer, and producer

1945 Gabe Kaplan; actor, comedian

1948 Al Gore; 45th U.S. Vice President

1948 Rhea Perlman; Emmy Award-winning actress

1950 Ed Marinaro; football, actor

1953 Sean Hopper; musician, keyboardist

1955 Angus Young; musician, guitarist

1957 Marc McClure; actor

1969 Steve Smith; basketball

1971 Ewan McGregor; actor

1971 Pavel Bure; hockey

EVENTS FOR MARCH 31st

1492 – As a directive of the Alhambra Decree, Jews in Spain were given three months to accept Christianity or leave.

1880 - The first electric streetlights installed by a municipality were turned on in Wabash, Indiana.

The Eiffel Tower in a picture taken by Brian Tibbets, October 2007. Public domain

1889 – The Eiffel Tower in Paris was inaugurated.

1896 – Whitcomb L. Judson from Chicago, Illinois patented the hookless shoe fastener.

1900 - The W.E. Roach Company became the first automobile company to advertise in a national magazine when they advertised "Automobiles that Give Satisfaction" in the *Saturday Evening Post*.

1909 – Construction began on a boat that the publication *The Shipbuilder and Marine Engine Builder* described as being "virtually unsinkable." The new boat in construction: the RMS *Titanic*.

1912 – Construction was completed on the RMS *Titanic*.

1917 - The United States purchase of the Danish West Indies for $25 million, agreed to the previous August, took effect. They called them the Virgin Islands.

1918 - Daylight Saving Time went into effect throughout the United States. People sprung ahead an hour, allowing for longer early evenings.

1930 – The Motion Pictures Production Code was instituted, imposing strict guidelines on the treatment of sex, crime, religion and violence in film. It remained in effect in the U.S. for the next thirty-eight years.

1931 - The great Knute Rockne died in a plane crash during a flight from Kansas City to Los Angeles where he was supposed to take part in the film *The Spirit of Notre Dame*.

1939 - British Prime Minister Neville Chamberlain undertook to defend Poland in an Anglo-French alliance if attacked.

1943 - The musical *Oklahoma!* opened on Broadway. Gossip columnist Walter Winchell originally predicted failure for the new musical by writing "No girls. No legs. No chance." After 2,212 performances, it would seem Winchell was incorrect.

1949 - Newfoundland joined the Canadian Federation as the nation's 10th province.

A far cry from the present day PC, this is the UNIVAC I control station in the Museum of Science; Boston, Massachusetts. Public domain.

1951 – Remington Rand delivered the first UNIVAC I computer to the United States Census Bureau.

1959 - The 14th Dalai Lama, fleeing Chinese repression of an uprising in Tibet, arrived at the Indian border and was granted political asylum.

1962 – "Soldier Boy," recorded by the female group The Shirelles, entered Billboard's pop record charts. Less than a month later, the song would enjoy a three-week stay in the #1 spot.

1968 - United States President Lyndon Johnson announced he would not run for re-election.

1969 - Delacorte Press published Kurt Vonnegut's novel, *Slaughterhouse Five.*

1969 - George and Patti Harrison were fined $1,200 for possession of marijuana. Harrison maintained that the raid, which occurred a month earlier, was a frame-up by police.

1973 - Ken Norton beat Muhammad Ali in a 12-round split decision, during which Ali had his jaw broken.

1973 - Stevie Wonder's recording of "You Are the Sunshine of My Life" entered the pop charts. It was on the charts for 13 weeks and was #1 for one week.

1979 - The military relationship between Britain and Malta ended after 181 years with the departure of the destroyer HMS *London* from Valetta Harbour.

1983 - The Colombian city of Popayán was devastated by an earthquake which killed at least 500 people and left more than 3,000 homeless.

1985 – The first *WrestleMania*, the biggest wrestling event from the WWE, took place in Madison Square Garden in New York. The main event featured Hulk Hogan and Mr. T competing against Roddy Piper and Paul Orndorff. (Hogan and T were declared the winners.)

1985 - Nashville, Tennessee's "Tootsie's Orchid Lounge," a favorite of country music stars, closed. Four months after Tootsie's closed, the owner of the building filed paperwork to register the name "World Famous Tootsie's Orchid Lounge." Tootsie's son sued to have the rights of the name returned to him and lost. The building was leased out in August of 1985 and reopened under the new name.

1986 - A Mexicana Airlines Boeing 727 crashed into a mountainside in central Mexico en route from Mexico City to Los Angeles. All 166 people were killed.

1987 - HBO earned its first Oscar for *Down and Out in America*.

1990 - A rally against a new and unpopular poll tax turned into a violent riot in the heart of London.

1991 - Former child actor and radio personality Danny Bonaduce was arrested for the beating and robbery of Darius Lee Barney, a transvestite prostitute.

1991 - After 36 years in existence, the Warsaw Pact, the military alliance between the Soviet Union and its eastern European satellites, came to an end.

The third USS *Missouri* ("Mighty Mo" or "Big Mo") is a U.S. Navy battleship, notable as the final battleship to be built by the United States and the site of the Japanese surrender at the end of World War II. Public domain.

1992 – The USS *Missouri* was decommissioned in Long Beach, California

1993 - Brandon Lee, the son of the late martial-arts star Bruce Lee, was killed during filming of *The Crow* in Wilmington, North Carolina.

1995 - All 60 people aboard a Romanian Tarom airlines Airbus were killed when it crashed and burst into flames shortly after takeoff for Brussels.

1998 – Netscape released the code base of its browser under an open-source license agreement; the project was given the code name "Mozilla" and is eventually spun off into the non-profit Mozilla Foundation.

1999 - *The Matrix*, starring Keanu Reeves and Laurence Fishburne, opened in United States theaters.

2004 – In Fallujah, Iraq, 4 American private military contractors working for Blackwater USA, were killed and their bodies mutilated after being ambushed.

2008 – Aloha Airlines, a bankrupt airline, permanently ended passenger service

Attributions

Assigning attributions to each morsel of information in a work such as this is, to say the least, a daunting task. True enough, the Internet played a role in research, but it wasn't the only source of information.

At the time of this writing, the word "trivia" was entered into the "search string" on Google. In less than a second, the search engine returned 107 *million* results! To have used nothing but the Internet to confirm these pieces of information would have taken countless hours to churn out ounces of data laced with pounds of errors. A casual comparison between the trivia-based websites will reveal that much of the information had been copied word-for-word from one site to the next. Because of the large number of trivia sites, it is safe to assume that much of the data was copied without verification. The end result was a collection of inaccuracies that were passed from source to source like a harmful virus spreading from host to host.

So, is a claim being made here that every sentence of information in this book is accurate? Yes…to a point. If a statement found was reflected only within trivia, unsupported, or unverifiable sites, it was not included in this work. The only data in this collection are those that could be found in other sources besides trivia sites and, in many cases, external references such as books, magazines, etc.

And then there are the events that occurred to which we were all witness, either through the media or by first-hand experience. These are the best because they are the most reliable.

Even though research has been done to confirm everything found within these covers, the reader is urged to use them at his or her own risk. This book should not be taken as the final word for serious research, but rather a simple companion for light reading, designed to cause a reader to proclaim, "*I'll be darned.*" Use this for conversations at work, dinner table discussions, or for icebreakers. But for serious, detailed research, go to the library.

That being said, here is a list of sources used to compile data for *The Book of March*:

WEB SITES

http://articles.cnn.com

http://news.bbc.co.uk

http://sportsillustrated.cnn.com

http://thegreatgeekmanual.com

http://www.aahn.org/

http://www.alyeska-pipe.com

http://www.bartleby.com

http://www.bmwcoop.com

http://www.britannica.com

http://www.history.com/

http://www.imdb.com

http://www.indiana.edu

http://www.itnsource.com/

http://www.law.cornell.edu

http://www.nytimes.com

http://www.offthepace.com

http://www.parliament.vic.gov.au

http://www.redcross.org

http://www.riaa.com

http://www.tv.com

http://www.uspto.gov/

http://www.wikipedia.org/

http://www.wired.com

BOOKS AND PUBLICATIONS

1816: America Rising by Carl Edward Skeen (book)

1968 in Europe: a History of Protest and Activism, 1956-1977 by Martin Klimke, Joachim Scharloth (book)

A Reference Guide to Latin American History by James D. Henderson, Helen Delpar, Maurice Philip Brungardt, Richard N. Weldon (book)

A stitch In Time: a Baseball Chronology by Gene Elston (book)

Across the Taiwan Strait: Mainland China, Taiwan, and the 1995-1996 Crisis by Suisheng Zhao (book)

Albert Einstein: Physicist & Genius by Lillian E. Forman (book)

American Minute by William J. Federer (book)

America's Forgotten Pandemic: the Influenza of 1918 by Alfred W. Crosby (book)

Annual Report, 1996, Part 3 by International Monetary Fund (report)

Asad in Search of Legitimacy: Message and Rhetoric in the Syrian Press by Mordechai Kedar (book)

Ballroom, Boogie, Shimmy Sham, Shake: a Social and Popular Dance Reader by Julie Malnig (book)

Baseball Digest Mar 1990 (magazine)

Baseball Digest Mar 1998 (magazine)

Bing Crosby: Crooner of the Century by Richard Grudens (book)

Bismarck: The Man & the Statesman, Volume 2 by Otto Von Bismarck (book)

Blobson's Dire Mishaps in a Barn Storming Company by Mortimer Shelley (book)

Breakdown, Breakup, Breakthrough: Germany's Difficult Passage to Modernity by Carl F. Lankowski, Andrei S. Markovits (book)

Bulletin of the Atomic Scientists Jan 1985 (periodical)

Care of the Aged, The by Isaac Max Rubinow, University of Chicago. Graduate School of Social Service Administration (book)

China's Rise, Taiwan's Dilemmas and International Peace by Edward Friedman (book)

Chronology and Index of the Second World War, 1938-1945 by Royal Institute of International Affairs

Chronology; or, The Historian's Companion by Thomas Tegg (book)

Civil Wars of the World by Karl R. DeRouen

Collected Works of Abraham Lincoln, Volume 2, The by Abraham Lincoln (book)

Colombia: Essays on Conflict, Peace, and Development by Andrés Solimano (book)

Columbia Chronologies of Asian History and Culture by John Stewart Bowman (book)

Conflict, Cleavage, and Change in Central Asia and the Caucasus by Karen Dawisha, Bruce Parrott (book)

Crime Classification Manual: a Standard System for Investigating and Classifying Violent Crimes by John E. Douglas, Ann W. Burgess, Allen G. Burgess, Robert K. Ressler (book)

Daily Life During the Holocaust by Eve Nussbaum Soumerai, Carol D. Schulz (book)

Dazed and Confused: Teenage Nostalgia. Instant and Cool 70's Memorabilia by Richard Linklater (book)

Development and Disorder: a History of the Third World Since 1945 by Michael G. Mason, Mike Mason (book)

Emporium of Arts and Sciences, Volume 1 By Thomas Cooper (book)

Enabling: Webster's Quotations, Facts and Phrases by Inc Icon Group International (book)

Encyclopaedia Britannica/Getty Images History of the World In Photographs, The by Encyclopaedia Britannica, Getty Images (book)

Encyclopedia of Terrorist, Natural, and Man-Made Disasters by Michael I. Greenberg (book)

Engineering & Contracting, Volume 63, Issues 5-6 by Halbert Powers Gillette (periodical)

Entertainment Celebrities by Norbert B. Laufenberg (book)

Europe Since 1945 by Philip Malcolm Waller Thody (book)

Every-Day-Of-The-School-Year Math Problems by Marcia Miller, Martin Lee

Failure Is Impossible!: the History of American Women's Rights by Martha E. Kendall (book)

Famous Male Athletes: Grades 4-8 by R. Solski (Book)

George Eastman: Founder of Kodak and the Photography Business by Carl W. Ackerman (book)

Handy Politics Answer Book, The by Gina Misiroglu (book)

Harvard Century: The Making of a University to a Nation, The by Richard Norton Smith (book)

Harvard Illustrated Magazine, The, Volume 9 (magazine)

History of the American Steam Fire-Engine by William T. King (book)

Hollywood Songsters: Garland to O'Connor by James Robert Parish, Michael R. Pitts (book)

How America Saved the World by Eric Hammel (book)

I Like Being Married: Treasured Traditions, Rituals and Stories by Michael Leach, Therese Johnson Borchard (book)

Imperfect Union: Constitutional Structures of German Unification, The by Peter E. Quint (book)

India, GCC and the Global Energy Regime by Samir Ranjan Pradhan (book)

Indiana, an Interpretation by John Bartlow Martin (book)

Indo-Russian Relations: Prospects, Problems, and Russia Today by V. D. Chopra, International Institute for Asia-Pacific Studies (book)

Invasion of Kuwait, The by John King, Andrew Nancy Irani Laur Irani Laur King, John King (book)

Jazz Singers: the Ultimate Guide, The by Scott Yanow (book)

Jim Bakker: Miscarriage of Justice? by James A. Albert (book)

JOSEPH ONCALE, PETITIONER v. SUNDOWNER OFFSHORE SERVICES, INCORPORATED, et al. (Supreme Court Document)

Joseph Smith and the Origins of the Book of Mormon by David Persuitte (book)

Juvenile Justice: The Essentials by Mario L. Hesse, Mario Hesse, Richard Lawrence (book)

King Kong: the History of a Movie Icon From Fay Wray to Peter Jackson by Ray Morton (book)

Liberty Spring 1973 (magazine)

Lincolnshire by Edward Mansel Sympson (book)

Mother Jones Magazine May-Jun 1995 (magazine)

Movies That Changed Us, The: Reflections on the Screen by Nick Clooney (book)

Mr. Lincoln and His War by John Griffin (book)

National Game, The by Alfred Henry Spink (book)

National Wrestling Alliance: The Untold Story of the Monopoly That Strangled Pro Wrestling by Tim Hornbaker (book)

NATO Enlargement Debate, 1990-1997: Blessings of Liberty, The by Gerald B. H. Solomon, Center for Strategic and International Studies (book)

Nazi Olympics, The by Richard D. Mandell (book)

New Iranian Leadership, The by Yonah Alexander, Milton M. Hoenig (book)

Niagara Falls by Sarah Tieck (book)

No Cross, No Crown by William Penn (book)

On the Air: the Encyclopedia of Old-Time Radio by John Dunning (book)

On This Date: A Day-by-Day Look at Historical Events by Brian Merrill (book)

Oxford Companion to American Food and Drink, The by Andrew F. Smith (book)

Politics of Regional Integration in Latin America, The by Olivier Dabène (book)

Popular Science Jun 1962 (magazine)

Predicting New Words: The Secrets of Their Success by Allan A. Metcalf (book)

Prompt a Day!: 625 Thought-Provoking Writing Prompts Linked to Every Day of the Year by Jacqueline Sweeney (book)

Public Diary of President Sadat, The by Raphael Israeli (book)

Read the Beatles: Classic and New Writings on the Beatles, Their Legacy, and Why They Still Matter by June Skinner Sawyers, Astrid Kirchherr (book)

Reclaiming History: the Assassination of President John F. Kennedy by Vincent Bugliosi

Republic of Drivers: a Cultural History of Automobility in America by Cotten Seiler (book)

Rimbaud and Jim Morrison: the Rebel as Poet by Wallace Fowlie (book)

Rise and Fall of the Communist Party of Burma, The (CPB) by Bertil Lintner (book)

Romantic Revolutions: Criticism and Theory by Kenneth R. Johnston (book)

Safire's Political Dictionary by William Safire (book)

Save Women's Lives: History of Washing Machines by Lee M. Maxwell (book)

Separation of Church and State in the United States by Alvin W. Johnson, Frank H. Yost (book)

Simeon North, First Official Pistol Maker of the United States: a Memoir by Simon Newton Dexter North, Ralph H. North (book)

Tales from the Chicago Blackhawks by Harvey Wittenberg (book)

Terrorism, 1992-1995 by Edward F. Mickolus, Susan L. Simmons (book)

The ABC Movie of the Week Companion: A Loving Tribute to the Classic Series by Michael Karol (book)

The Great Pictorial History of World Crime by Jay Robert Nash (book)

The Life of Franz Schubert, Volume 2 by Heinrich Kreissle von Hellborn, Heinrich von Kreissle, Sir George Grove (book)

The New York Times (newspaper)

The Unreleased Beatles: Music & Film by Richie Unterberger (book)

Then Is Now by Cheryl Dangel Cullen (book)

Then Sings My Soul: 150 of the World's Greatest Hymn Stories by Robert J. Morgan (book)

Thomas Jefferson by Heidi M. D. Elston (book)

Total football: the Official Encyclopedia of the National Football League by Bob Carroll (book)

Ulysses S. Grant: An Album: Warrior, Husband, Traveler, Emancipator, Writer by William S. McFeely, Neil Giordano (book)

United Kingdumb: Idiots from the British Isles by Leland Gregory (book)

United States in the First World War, The: an Encyclopedia by Anne Cipriano Venzon, Paul L. Miles (book)

Wallace's Monthly, Volume 19 by John Hankins Wallace (magazine circa 1893)

Watching TV: six decades of American Television by Harry Castleman, Walter J. Podrazik (book)

What Risk? by Roger Bate (book)

Young Henry Ford: a Picture History of the First Forty Years by Sidney Olson (book)

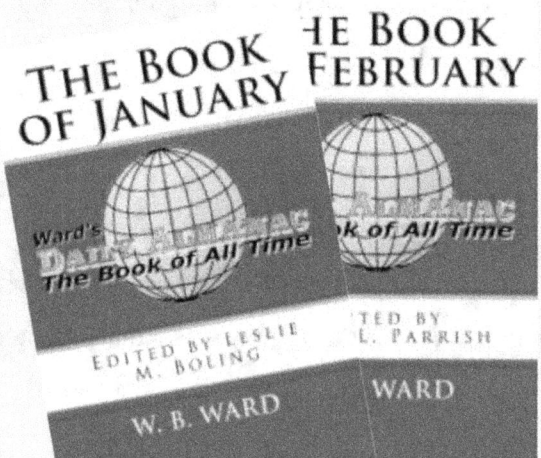

www.ingramcontent.com/pod-product-compliance
Lightning Source LLC
Chambersburg PA
CBHW081346280526
45788CB00009B/2791